31 DAY SPIRITUAL MINDSET MAKEOVER

A Journey Through The Book of Proverbs

Carlene B. Charlemagne

The opinions expressed in this manuscript are solely the opinions of the author and do not represent the opinions or thoughts of the publisher. The author has represented and warranted full ownership and/or legal right to publish all the materials in this book.

31 Day Spiritual Mindset Makeover
A Journey Through The Book of Proverbs
All Rights Reserved.
Copyright © 2013 Carlene B. Charlemagne
v5.0

Cover Photo © 2013 JupiterImages Corporation.
All rights reserved - used with permission.

This book may not be reproduced, transmitted, or stored in whole or in part by any means, including graphic, electronic, or mechanical without the express written consent of the publisher except in the case of brief quotations embodied in critical articles and reviews.

This journal or parts thereof may not be reproduced in parts or whole, in any form, stored in a retrieval system, or transmitted in any form by any means—electronic, mechanical, photocopy, recording, or otherwise—without prior written permission from the author, without written permission, except in the case of reprint in the context of reviews and as provided by United States of America copyright law.

Scripture taken from the HOLY BIBLE, NEW INTERNATIONAL VERSION®. Copyright © 1973, 1978, 1984 by International Bible Society. Used by permission of Zondervan, All rights Reserved.

The "NIV" and "New International Version" trademarks are registered in the United States Patent and Trademark Office by International Bible Society. Use of either trademark requires the permission of International Bible Society.

Outskirts Press, Inc.
http://www.outskirtspress.com

ISBN: 978-1-4787-1190-2

Library of Congress Control Number: 2013902330

Outskirts Press and the "OP" logo are trademarks belonging to Outskirts Press, Inc.

PRINTED IN THE UNITED STATES OF AMERICA

Acknowledgments

I want to thank God for trusting me with this important assignment that will help transform the lives of millions. I give thanks to the Holy Spirit for leading me daily as I put into practice what I wrote, even when I wanted to give up. He showed me my purpose in the Kingdom, which was worth all the trials and challenges that I encountered during this project.

I want to thank my husband Dwayne Eddings and our children Michael, Daniel, David, Keiyana, and Kyra for inspiring me. I want to thank Karen Morales and Printing Delite, Inc. for doing a wonderful job on The Power of "I AM" poster and the 365-Day Bible Reading Plan. Special thanks to Outskirts Press and its wonderful team of professionals for delivering the final product.

I want to thank Golda Watts for her editing contributions and Angela Barfield (Miracle Message Wear - Halo Dezigns) for her proofreading skills. Thanks to all my friends, families, and business partners that made contributions as well as empowering me during this project.

Last but not least, I want to thank Barry Donaldson (MMG Marketing) for his profound words "Get your mind right." Also special thanks to John Marques (Muscle Maker Restaurants) for keeping my temple healthy as well as believing in my ministry and partnering with me to take this book to the masses.

Proverbs is the book of heavenly wisdom for daily living. With over 900 inspired precepts, the Book of Proverbs provides godly counsel for every area of human experience and relationship. The maxims deal with wisdom and folly, initiatives and laziness, prosperity and poverty, humility and pride, love and lust, justice and vengeance, friends and enemies, masters and servants, life and death, anger and anxieties, leaders and followers, and much, much more.

This journal is designed to help you spend focused time to acquire daily wisdom. After all, Proverbs is the Book of Wisdom. There is a chapter for each day of the month. At the end of each month, you can start all over again and have the self-evident experience of gaining more wisdom. Just think how spiritually smart you will become when you make this book a daily part of your spiritual walk.

Proverbs deals with virtually every area of living. I believe that it will help you examine your life from a biblical perspective. Even though Proverbs is found in the Old Testament, its counsels are still valid and are very much needed today. If you follow the precepts, they will help you to model your everyday living to become what God expects of you.

Outlined in this workbook are 31 days of inspiration from the Word of God. The workbook will put you on a journey to a **Spiritual Mindset Makeover**, which will propel you into a life of Spiritual Boldness.

Each day you spend applying these biblical truths, you will receive a personal revelation that will change your life for the better. It is a proven system that will produce long-lasting results that will manifest in every area of your life: spiritually, emotionally, physically, relationally, and financially. This journal will guide you daily as you apply Heavenly Wisdom to your earthly walk.

Let's face it: your way of thinking has created your past and present, and it will create your future. If the life that you are living right now is not the one you desire, then your thinking has to change and line up with the Word of God. Your thoughts produce life or death, and have the ability to give positive or negative power to your words, behaviors, and actions. Your thoughts have the power to release or limit God's ability into your life.

In order to receive the fullness of His Blessings, you have to learn how to renew your mind daily with the Word of God so that you can experience what it means to Live Life Unlimited. *(Be sure to journal your experiences daily. When you review your journal periodically, you will have firsthand evidence of the remarkable changes in your life from month to month as you continuously spend time with God.)*

"Whatever is true, whatever is noble, whatever is right, whatever is pure, whatever is lovely, whatever is admirable—if anything is excellent or praiseworthy—think about such things." (Philippians 4:8-9 [NIV])

Introduction

Spiritual Mindset is a term that I coined to help me stay focused on my journey to greatness. As I started delving into the Word of God for guidance, He revealed something to me that changed my life and my beliefs forever. I want to share some of the things that I learned from the Creator Himself, and I hope you can apply these truths to change your life as well.

I understood that I was in this world but not of this world, so I had to do things differently. I started changing my thinking about life and how I pursued success. I had to transform my mind from a carnal to a spiritual mindset with the help of God and His Word. By doing so, I made God my guide and started meditating upon His Word. It took a few years to get to where I am, but I held God and myself accountable for my success.

What I have learned is that the Only One who can take you from where you are to the place that you were born to be in the shortest period of time is the One Himself who created you. Sure, many authors have written books about their life's journey to help us, but I believe everyone has their own journey to complete. We can get insight from others to help us stay motivated on our walk, but no one but God can tell us to the last detail what we must do to fulfill our destiny.

I did not set out to write a book. I simply set out on a journey of truth and self-discovery. I hope that what I have learned will help you stay focused as well as motivated on your journey to greatness. My hope is that no matter where you are in your life journey, you will not give up. You have two choices. You can use the experiences of others to help shorten your learning curve, or you can learn from your own experiences. It might take a little longer, but I promise that if you give control to God, your steps will be guided and your life's journey will be a testimony that will help guide the life of others.

The Holy Spirit told me to write this journal on **Spiritual Mindset**. The instructions were to use the wisdom based on the Book of Proverbs. I was instructed to write a chapter a day for 31 days. As I started writing the book, I was flooded with information daily that I knew could come only from God. At one point, I let fear get the best of me because I did not believe that I could write a book in 31 days since writing a book often takes months or years to complete.

The Lord dealt with me to get me back in the spiritual zone to finish my assignment. At that point, I was writing 3-4 chapters daily to keep up with the 31-day deadline. After my part was completed, God sent the helpers to finalize this book so it could be launched on Easter 2013.

This book is a road map for anyone who is tired of living year after year with no fulfilling purpose in his or her life. It is for the person who makes resolutions every year just to fail because they lack accountability. This book puts the accountability on you and God. Together you are a team, and that's all you need to begin your journey to greatness.

He will convict you when you stray off course. Some days will be more difficult than others, but I promise that if you make this a daily part of your walk, you will see transformation within the first 30 days. God said in His Word that "He will never leave you nor forsake you" (Deuteronomy 31:6), but be careful that you do not give up on you, because He never will. If you continue to be accountable to yourself and Him, I promise that you will be transformed in every area of your life by the following year.

How to Use the Journal

Each day begins with "**Today's Reading**," which is the chapter of Proverbs that will be the focus. "**Today's Scripture**" is a thought-provoking verse, selected from the chapter, which will be the guiding light for the day. "**Today's Wisdom**" is the first step to moving the attention and thoughts to Godly Truths. "**Today's Spiritual Mindset**" takes the human condition and guides you through to the solution prescribed in the scripture verse.

Changing your perception and living your life based on a Spiritual Mindset begins with your courage to examine your life through the Word of God. The "**Spiritual Mindset Journal**" section is designed to help you unearth areas in your daily experiences that you want to change for the better. The results you receive will be based on how truthful you are with yourself.

There will be no benefit to this process if there are no solutions to the problems you have identified in your life. Therefore, the section "**Spiritual Mindset Action Plan**" is designed to help you make decisions and put into action daily activities that will propel you toward God's plan and purpose for your life. I also included **"The Power of I AM"** affirmations to help you affirm daily that you are what God says you are and you can do **all** that He says you can do. Additionally, I have included a "**365-day Bible Reading Plan**" calendar to help you delve deeper into the Word of God so you can read through the Bible in one year. Also available is a **Companion CD** to keep you motivated as you journey through this book. I will be with you daily as your accountability partner especially on those days when it seems like you are on the loosing end of your situation. I will be with you every step of the way encouraging and motivating you to greatness. The CD is additional and is available on this website www.spiritualmindset.net.

As you study and apply the Word daily, you will notice the subtle changes in your lifestyle. Within the first 30 days, you will be able to chart your progress from day 1 to day 30. Imagine the possibility of you taking your life from where you are to where you want to be in 30, 60, or 90 days from the day you started. The possibilities are endless, but nothing will be possible until you begin.

This unique journal will help you to:

- Develop a proven system that will move you steadily toward your goals.

- Empower yourself with the powerful affirmations of "I AM" to begin and end your day with an "I AM!" attitude.

- Organize and achieve your personal and professional goals with a daily accountability plan.

- Educate yourself on the powerful Word of God with the 365-Day Bible Reading Plan Calendar as you read through the bible in one year.

- Evaluate your progress by recording daily your achievements, successes, and strengths.

- Acquire powerful life changing habits that will build confidence as you embark on a journey of enlightenment.

DAY ONE

Today's Reading: **Proverbs Chapter 1**

The Proverbs of Solomon son of David, King of Israel: **2** for attaining wisdom and discipline; for understanding words of insight; **3** for acquiring a disciplined and prudent life, doing what is right and just and fair; **4** for giving prudence to the simple, knowledge and discretion to the young—**5** let the wise listen and add to their learning, and let the discerning get guidance—**6** for understanding proverbs and parables, the sayings and riddles of the wise. **7** The fear of the Lord is the beginning of knowledge, but fools despise wisdom and discipline. **8** Listen, my son, to your father's instruction and do not forsake your mother's teaching. **9** They will be a garland to grace your head and a chain to adorn your neck. **10** My son, if sinners entice you, do not give in to them. **11** If they say, "Come along with us; let's lie in wait for someone's blood, let's waylay some harmless soul; **12** Let's swallow them alive, like the grave, and whole, like those who go down to the pit; **13** We will get all sorts of valuable things and fill our houses with plunder; **14** throw in your lot with us, and we will share a common purse" – **15** my son, do not go along with them, do not set foot on their paths; **16** for their feet rush into sin, they are swift to shed blood. **17** How useless to spread a net in full view of all the birds! **18** These men lie in wait for their own blood; they waylay only themselves! **19** Such is the end of all who go after ill-gotten gain; it takes away the lives of those who get it. **20** Wisdom calls aloud in the street, she raises her voice in the public squares; **21** at the head of the noisy streets she cries out, in the gateways of the city she makes her speech: **22** "How long will you simple ones love your simple ways? How long will mockers delight in mockery and fools hate knowledge?

23 If you had responded to my rebuke, I would have poured out my heart to you and made my thoughts known to you. **24** But since you rejected me when I called and no one gave heed when I stretched out my hand, **25** since you ignored all my advice and would not accept my rebuke, **26** I in turn will laugh at your disaster; I will mock when calamity overtakes you - **27** when calamity overtakes you like a storm, when disaster sweeps over you like a whirlwind, when distress and trouble overwhelm you. **28** "Then they will call to me but I will not answer; they will look for me but will not find me. **29** Since they hated knowledge and did not choose to fear the Lord, **30** since they would not accept my advice and spurned my rebuke, **31** they will eat the fruit of their ways and be filled with the fruit of their schemes. **32** For the waywardness of the simple will kill them, and the complacency of fools will destroy them; **33** but whoever listens to me will live in safety and be at ease, without fear of harm."

Today's Scripture: "The fear of the Lord is the beginning of knowledge, but fools despise wisdom and discipline." (Proverbs 1:7)

Today's Wisdom: The opposite of faith is fear. In order to overcome fear, you must strengthen your faith in God and His ability to work through us.

Today's Spiritual Mindset: God tells us in His Word that greater is He that is in us than he that is in the world. That should be more than enough to take us to the highest levels of success in our lives, but most people believe the opposite. Their fear keeps them stuck where they are and makes them unable to move forward in fulfilling their goals and dreams. They fear failure, they fear success, they fear what people are going to say or think about them, and they even feel fear because of their lack of confidence in themselves. Without faith, it is impossible to please God, so you have to ask God to help you overcome any fears that are stopping you from pursuing the calling that He has placed on your life.

Spiritual Mindset Journal: Fear is an emotion that has been pre-programmed into animals and humans as an instinctual response to potential danger. Such is the fear of rattlesnakes, or a bear, or anything that can cause us harm or possible death. However, when fear has you immobilized by excessive worry and you begin to fear events that have not happened, then it is time to commit your fears and worries to God in prayer. He is the only One that can release you from fear and anxiety, and free you to realistically deal with your needs and welfare as well as the needs and welfare of others.

Use the workspace below to list at least three (3) times in your life that fear has prevented you from moving forward to pursue opportunities in life.

_____
_____
_____
_____
_____
_____
_____
_____
_____
_____
_____
_____
_____
_____
_____
_____
_____
_____
_____
_____

Spiritual Mindset Action Plan: No one is living at their best if he or she is not living at their best spiritually. Today you will begin your journey of change from a carnal mindset to a Spiritual Mindset -- from a mindset controlled by fear to a mindset that is constantly renewed by your faith. The person with a carnal mind thinks differently from a person who is spiritually grounded. Life at times can be difficult, but it is your spiritual thinking that will help you to overcome your fears and challenges daily, as you develop yourself to greatness.

The first step is to delve into the Word of God to seek wisdom and understanding. Today, begin to apply the Word to every area of your life as the opportunity presents itself. Renewing your mind is the first step to transformation and restoration. Whatever comes up against you, instead of confessing death, speak life into your situations.

For example, if you got up this morning not feeling well, then confess that you are healed. If your wallet does not represent prosperity, then confess that you are rich. If you feel fear creeping in to hold you back, then confess that you are walking in Holy Ghost boldness. It is when you meditate on the Word that it takes root in your heart. When the Word of God is rooted and grounded in your spirit, thoughts, words, and actions begin to line up with God's will for your life, and the **Spiritual Mindset** begins to transform you from the inside out.

Day One Worksheet

1. What mindset changes did you experience?

2. What kind of spiritual breakthroughs did you have based on your decision to walk in faith?

3. How can you be an example to others now that you know you have power over fear?

_____
_____
_____
_____
_____
_____
_____
_____
_____
_____
_____
_____
_____
_____
_____
_____
_____
_____
_____
_____
_____
_____
_____
_____

Notes

Notes

Notes

DAY TWO

Today's Reading: Proverbs Chapter 2

My son, if you accept my words and store up my commands within you, **2** turning your ear to wisdom and applying your heart to understanding, **3** and if you call out for insight and cry aloud for understanding, **4** and if you look for it as for silver and search for it as for hidden treasure, **5** then you will understand the fear of the Lord and find the knowledge of God. **6** For the Lord gives wisdom, and from his mouth come knowledge and understanding. **7** He holds victory in store for the upright, he is a shield to those whose walk is blameless, **8** for he guards the course of the just and protects the way of his faithful ones. **9** Then you will understand what is right and just and fair – every good path. **10** For wisdom will enter your heart, and knowledge will be pleasant to your soul. **11** Discretion will protect you, and understanding will guard you. **12** Wisdom will save you from the ways of wicked men, from men whose words are perverse, **13** who leave the straight paths to walk in dark ways, **14** who delight in doing wrong and rejoice in the perverseness of evil, **15** whose paths are crooked and who are devious in their ways. **16** It will save you also from the adulteress, from the wayward wife with her seductive words, **17** who has left the partner of her youth and ignored the covenant she made before God. **18** For her house leads down to death and her paths to the spirits of the dead. **19** None who go to her return or attain the paths of life. **20** Thus you will walk in the ways of good men and keep to the paths of the righteous. **21** For the upright will live in the land, and the blameless will remain in it; **22** but the wicked will be cut off from the land, and the unfaithful will be torn from it.

Today's Scripture: "He holds victory in store for the upright; he is a shield to those whose walk is blameless." (Proverbs 2:7)

Today's Wisdom: People do not make plans to end their lives in ruin, but many lives are ruined by people's earthly plans. We write the plans but it is God who rights our plans.

Today's Spiritual Mindset: What is God's plan and purpose for your life? If you do not know, all you have to do is ASK. "Why am I here?" is a question that you should know the answer to; if you do not, then you may be living a life that is not in alignment with God's plan and purpose for you.

Spiritual Mindset Journal: The enemy is alive and well...and craftily cunning in his attempt to destroy the plans that God has for His children. Do not be a victim of his devices. He is like a fisherman who baits his hook according to the appetite of the fish. Will you get caught on his hook?

Use the workspace below to list at least three (3) negative habits (appetites) that you want to change for the better.

_____
_____
_____
_____
_____
_____
_____
_____
_____
_____
_____
_____

_____
_____
_____
_____
_____
_____
_____
_____

Spiritual Mindset Action Plan: What is the enemy using to distract you from the plans that God has for you on your journey to greatness? There is a lot of development that you have to go through to prepare you for the great things that God has planned for your life. The enemy wants you to give up. He wants you to quit. He wants you to throw in the towel. He tries to convince you that the challenges that you are going through mean that God has abandoned you. He is deceiving you and telling you that God does not care about you or your future, when in actuality it is quite the opposite. God has a hope and a future for you. (Jeremiah 29:11)

If He gives you His Blessings before you are ready to receive them, you will not have the necessary virtues to be the custodian of the Blessings with their coexisting Wisdom to selflessly share them with others. You will become even more selfish, and that will please the enemy because you never became what God wanted you to be. But if you trust in God and in the power of His Might, you can turn off the voice of the enemy and tune in to God's Voice through the power of His Word.

Trust Him and what He says. Do not fight or challenge your development, or the process that He is taking you through. Embrace your challenges and thank Him for the perfect solution. Know that God is there with you right in the midst of your situations. As you overcome the challenges and learn the lessons, you will see a beautiful and fulfilling life unfold before you.

Day Two Worksheet

1. What challenges are you facing today?

2. What reasons (excuses) are you giving for not progressing through these experiences?

3. How did your challenges change when you acknowledged God and His Perfect plan?

Notes

Notes

DAY THREE

Today's Reading: **Proverbs Chapter 3**

My son, do not forget my teachings, but keep my commands in your heart, **2** for they will prolong your life many years and bring you prosperity. **3** Let love and faithfulness never leave you; bind them around your neck, write them on the tablet of your heart. **4** Then you will win favor and a good name in the sight of God and man. **5** Trust in the Lord with all your heart and lean not on your own understanding; **6** in all your ways acknowledge him, and he will make your paths straight. **7** Do not be wise in your own eyes; fear the Lord and shun evil. **8** This will bring health to your body and nourishment to your bones. **9** Honor the Lord with your wealth, with the firstfruits of all your crops; **10** then your barn will be filled to overflowing, and your vats will brim over with new wine. **11** My son, do not despise the Lord's discipline and do not resent his rebuke, **12** because the Lord disciplines those he loves, as a father the son he delights in. **13** Blessed is the man who finds wisdom, the man who gains understanding, **14** for she is more profitable than silver and yields better returns than gold. **15** She is more precious than rubies; nothing you desire can compare with her. **16** Long life is in her right hand; in her left hand are riches and honor. **17** Her ways are pleasant ways, and all her paths are peace. **18** She is a tree of life to those who embrace her; those who lay hold of her will be blessed. **19** By wisdom the Lord laid the earth's foundations, by understanding he set the heavens in place; **20** by his knowledge the deeps were divided, and the clouds let drop the dew. **21** My son, preserve sound judgment and discernment, do not let them out of your sight; **22** they will be life for you, an ornament to grace your neck. **23** Then you will go on your way in safety, and your foot will not stumble; **24** when you lie down, you will not be afraid; when you lie down, your sleep will be sweet. **25** Have no fear of sudden disaster or of the ruin that overtakes the wicked, **26** for the Lord will be your confidence and will keep your foot from being snared. **27** Do not withhold good from those who deserve it, when it is in your power to act. **28** Do not say to your neighbor, "Come back later; I'll give it tomorrow"- when you now have it with you. **29** Do not plot harm against your neighbor, who lives trustfully near you. **30** Do not accuse a man for no reason- when he has done you no harm. **31** Do not envy a violent man or choose any of his ways, **32** for the Lord detests a perverse man but takes the upright into his confidence. **33** The Lord's curse is on the house of the wicked, but he blesses the home of the righteous. **34** He mocks proud mockers but gives grace to the humble. **35** The wise inherit honor, but fools he holds up to shame.

Today's Scripture: "Trust in the Lord with all your heart and lean not on your understanding." (Proverbs 3:5)

Today's Wisdom: Do not make plans and then ask God to Bless them. When you trust God's plan for your life, it is already Blessed.

Today's Spiritual Mindset: Are you committing ALL your plans to the Lord and asking Him for guidance and direction in accomplishing those plans? If you are not...maybe today is a good day to start.

Spiritual Mindset Journal: If your attitude, thinking, and problem-solving practices have been "When all else have failed, then I will turn to God for help," you are using God as a last resort. You are putting persons, places, conditions, and things before God when you do not trust in Him first.

Use the workspace below to record a problem that you had when you looked to other people for solutions before you trusted God. What were some of the solutions given by those persons you trusted? How many more problems sprouted as a result of trusting in other people?

_____
_____
_____
_____
_____
_____
_____
_____
_____
_____
_____
_____
_____
_____
_____
_____
_____
_____
_____
_____
_____
_____
_____
_____
_____
_____
_____
_____
_____

Spiritual Mindset Action Plan: Commit your plans to the Lord today. Sometimes you go through life so anxious to achieve success that you make decisions that do no line up with the Word of God. You get involved in activities that God did not ordain, and you partner up with people that God did not send. Eventually, you realize that instead of getting on the path to success, you are headed down a path of failure and destruction. At that point, you start blaming God and everyone else for your bad decisions.

God wants you to succeed in everything that you put your hands to, but it is conditional that it is in line with the plan and purpose that He has for your life. How do you know that you are walking in alignment with God's plan and purpose for your life? When He uses your talents, skills, and experiences to bless you and those around you. How will you know that God ordained the journey that you are on? Ask yourself if what you are doing is self-serving, or is it Blessing others? God's purpose for your life **ALWAYS** Blesses others as well as advances His Kingdom.

Day Three Worksheet

1. List all the problems you are coping with today.

2. Acknowledge God as the perfect solution of these problems at least once an hour each day. This will not be difficult because they will consume your thoughts every moment of every day.

3. As each problem gets resolved, erase it from the list.

Notes

Notes

Notes

DAY FOUR

Today's Reading: Proverbs Chapter 4

Listen, my sons, to a father's instruction; pay attention and gain understanding. **2** I give you a sound learning, so do not forsake my teaching. **3** When I was a boy in my father's house, still tender, and an only child of my mother, **4** he taught me and said, "Lay hold of my words with all your heart; keep my commands and you will live. **5** Get wisdom, get understanding; do not forget my words or swerve from them. **6** Do not forsake wisdom, and she will protect you; love her, and she will watch over you. **7** Wisdom is supreme; therefore get wisdom. Though it cost all you have, get understanding. **8** Esteem her, and she will exalt you; embrace her, and she will honor you. **9** She will set a garland of grace on your head and present you with a crown of splendor." **10** Listen, my son, accept what I say, and the years of your life will be many. **11** I guide you in the way of wisdom and lead you along straight paths. **12** When you walk, your steps will not be hampered; when you run, you will not stumble. **13** Hold on to instruction, do not let it go; guard it well, for it is your life. **14** Do not set foot on the path of the wicked or walk in the way of evil men. **15** Avoid it, do not travel on it; turn from it and go on your way. **16** For they cannot sleep till they do evil; they are robbed of slumber till they make someone fall. **17** They eat the bread of wickedness and drink the wine of violence. **18** The path of the righteous is like the first gleam of dawn, shining ever brighter till the full light of day. **19** But the way of the wicked is like deep darkness; they do not know what makes them stumble. **20** My son, pay attention to what I say; listen closely to my words. **21** Do not let them out of your sight, keep them within your heart; **22** for they are life to those who find them and health to a man's whole body. **23** Above all else, guard your heart, for it is the wellspring of life. **24** Put away perversity from your mouth; keep corrupt talk far from your lips. **25** Let your eyes look straight ahead, fix your gaze directly before you. **26** Make level paths for your feet and take only ways that are firm. **27** Do not swerve to the right or the left; keep your foot from evil.

Today's Scripture: "Listen to the Father's instructions; pay attention and gain understanding." (Proverbs 4:1)

Today's Wisdom: Take hold of God's Word with all your heart; keep His commands and never stray from them, no matter what circumstances might come up against you.

Today's Spiritual Mindset: Stop making decisions and taking actions based on advice you solicit from others. Each person has an individualized inner voice, commonly referred to as a conscience. Each time you ignore or rationalize why you should go against the promptings of your inner voice, it recedes to the point where you no longer sense a prompting. Listen and follow the next prompting, and watch the results. Each person knows right from wrong. Your inner voice will never prompt you to do wrong.

Spiritual Mindset Journal: Get Wisdom and get understanding, because they will watch over you. Wisdom costs nothing, so ask God for Wisdom and thank Him daily for Wisdom to make the right decisions at the right time so the years of your life will be plenty. Think about past situations when you did not listen to your inner voice and took actions contrary to its prompting.

Use the workspace below to write the instruction you received. What steps did you take to convince yourself to contradict the prompting you received? What did it cost you?

Spiritual Mindset Action Plan: What are your plans for today? Have you taken time to ask God to act on your behalf no matter what the circumstance? Do you think that you have everything under control and do not need His help today? God says in His Word that we ought to ask, and it shall be given unto us. At times, we ask God for things and because we do not see it in the time frame that we expect, we decide that God really does not answer prayers.

When you pray and ask God for something, it is like submitting a request to a company. There are many departments or channels that your request must go through in order for you to get the correct answer. Just like God, there are many unseen situations that come up against your prayer after it has been answered. For example, when you pray and ask in Jesus' name and your prayer is in alignment to God's Word, Jesus goes to God on your behalf. Before that answer gets to you, there are many evil powers and principalities that are battling the Angels in the supernatural to hinder your answers from getting to you. As you are waiting, the enemy is trying to convince you that the delay means that God has denied your answer.

Sometimes, it takes a while before you receive your manifestation in the natural. However, that is why God asks that you have faith in Him and in the power of His might. You ask, He answers. Even if the answer takes some time getting through to you, God promises that He will never be late. He will always be on time to meet your needs.

Day Four Worksheet

God wants us to Ask for our daily bread. He says in His word that we should Ask, Seek, and Knock. Begin asking today. Know that your prayers are answered when you ask in line with the Word of God.

1. What are you asking for today? Are you asking God for patience to wait on His perfect best for your life?

2. Can you remember asking God for things in the past that you did not receive and later realize that it was held back for your good?

3. Write down three (3) instances when you ask God for something and when you received the answer, it was better than you imagined.

_____
_____
_____
_____
_____
_____
_____
_____
_____
_____
_____
_____
_____
_____
_____

Notes

Notes

Notes

DAY FIVE

Today's Reading: Proverbs Chapter 5

My son, pay attention to my wisdom, listen well to my words of insight, **2** that you may maintain discretion and your lips may preserve knowledge. **3** For the lips of an adulteress drip honey, and her speech is smoother than oil; **4** but in the end she is bitter as gall, sharp as a double-edge sword. **5** Her feet go down to death; her steps lead straight to the grave. **6** She gives no thought to the way of life; her paths are crooked, but she knows it not. **7** Now then, my sons, listen to me; do not turn aside from what I say. **8** Keep to a path far from her, do not go near the door of her house, **9** lest you give your best strength to others and your years to one who is cruel, **10** lest strangers feast on your wealth and your toil enrich another man's house. **11** At the end of your life you will groan, when your flesh and body are spent. **12** You will say, "How I hated discipline! How my heart spurned correction! **13** I would not obey my teachers or listen to my instructors. **14** I have come to the brink of utter ruin in the midst of the whole assembly." **15** Drink water from your own cistern, running water from your own well. **16** Should your springs overflow in the streets, your streams of water in the public squares? **17** Let them be yours alone, never to be shared with strangers. **18** May your fountain be blessed, and may you rejoice in the wife of your youth. **19** A loving doe, a graceful deer – may her breasts satisfy you always, may you ever be captivated by her love. **20** Why be captivated, my son, by an adulteress? Why embrace the bosom of another man's wife? **21** For a man's ways are in full view of the Lord, and he examines all his paths. **22** The evil deeds of a wicked man ensnare him; the cords of his sin hold him fast. **23** He will die for lack of discipline, led astray by his own great folly.

Today's Scripture: "For a man's ways are in full view of the Lord, and he examines all his paths." (Proverbs 5:21)

Today's Wisdom: The Lord sees everything that you do. Wherever you go, know that He is always keeping watch over you.

Today's Spiritual Mindset: O Lord, I commit my ways to You alone. Please examine my inner thoughts and help me to be disciplined in my walk with You.

Spiritual Mindset Journal: What are your thoughts today? Do you know that your thought forms your beliefs and your beliefs dictate your words and your words control your actions? What if your thoughts are negative? How will that affect your outcome today?

Use the workspace below to write an inner secret thought that you have not shared with anyone. If you acted on this thought and it was a negative action, ask God to forgive you and ask for the strength and wisdom not to repeat this mistake again.

Ask God to remove the cause and the effect of your actions. Then forgive yourself. Erase what you have written as an act of accepting God's forgiveness. Remember, there is nothing hidden from God.

_____
_____
_____
_____
_____
_____
_____
_____
_____
_____
_____
_____
_____
_____
_____
_____
_____
_____
_____
_____
_____
_____
_____
_____
_____
_____
_____

Spiritual Mindset Action Plan: Do you know that the average mind entertains over 10,000 thoughts daily? From the time that you wake up to the time that you go to sleep, your mind is thinking about things, good and bad. It is a fact that wherever the mind goes, the man or woman follows--or whatever you think about, you bring about. In actuality, you are creating your future right now at this very minute with the thought that you are entertaining.

If 90% of your thoughts are negative, then you have created a future that is against you, and success will never find you. Now that you know you have a part in your future and the life that you dream of, what kinds of thoughts will you entertain going forward?

Today is the first day of the rest of your life, and as long as you have breath in your body, you can undo all the damages that you have created with your thoughts. How do you begin? Simply by canceling the negative thoughts that you have created against you and your future.

Next, ask God to take control of your thoughts until you have full control over them. Begin to imagine the life that you dream of having, begin to see the person that you dreamt of becoming, begin to see that future that God has planned for you. As you begin to daydream, the images will connect to your spirit, and your words and actions will begin to line up to work for you and not against you. Do not ponder on things you have no control over. Do what is within your power and turn the rest over to the Lord. Ask Him to align your negative thoughts to His plan and purpose for your life today.

Day Five Worksheet

1. Describe the person you dream of becoming.

2. Write realistic steps that will help you achieve the goal of becoming that person.

3. Reward yourself for the process and the attainment of each step.

_____
_____
_____
_____
_____
_____
_____
_____
_____
_____
_____
_____
_____
_____
_____
_____
_____
_____
_____
_____
_____
_____
_____
_____

Notes

Notes

Notes

DAY SIX

Today's Reading: **Proverbs Chapter 6**

My son, if you have put up security for your neighbor, if you have struck hands in pledge for another, **2** if you have been trapped by what you said, ensnared by the words of your mouth, **3** then do this, my son, to free yourself, since you have fallen into your neighbor's hands: Go and humble yourself; press your plea with your neighbor! **4** Allow no sleep to your eyes, no slumber to your eyelids. **5** Free yourself, like a gazelle from the hand of the hunter, like a bird from the snare of the fowler. **6** Go to the ant, you sluggard; consider its ways and be wise! **7** It has no commander, no overseer or ruler, **8** yet it stores its provisions in summer and gathers its food at harvest. **9** How long will you lie there, you sluggard? When will you get up from your sleep? **10** A little sleep, a little slumber, a little folding of the hands to rest—**11** and poverty will come on you like a bandit and scarcity like an armed man. **12** A scoundrel and villain, who goes about with a corrupt mouth, **13** who winks with his eye, signals with his feet and motions with his fingers, **14** who plots evil with deceit in his heart - he always stirs up dissension. **15** Therefore disasters will overtake him in an instant; he will suddenly be destroyed—without remedy. **16** There are six things the Lord hates, seven that are detestable to him: **17** haughty eyes, a lying tongue, hands that shed innocent blood, **18** a heart that devises wicked schemes, feet that are quick to rush into evil, **19** a false witness who pours out lies and a man who stirs up dissension among brothers. **20** My son, keep your father's commands and do not forsake your mother's teaching. **21** Bind them upon your heart forever; fasten them around your neck. **22**

When you walk, they will guide you; when you sleep, they will watch over you; when you awake, they will speak to you. **23** For these commands are a lamp, this teaching is a light, and the corrections of discipline are the way to life, **24** keeping you from the immoral woman, from the smooth tongue of the wayward wife. **25** Do not lust in your heart after her beauty or let her captivate you with her eyes, **26** for the prostitute reduces you to a loaf of bread, and the adulteress preys upon your very life. **27** Can a man scoop fire into his lap without his clothes being burned? **28** Can a man walk on hot coals without his feet being scorched? **29** So is he who sleeps with another man's wife; no one who touches her will go unpunished. **30** Men do not despise a thief if he steals to satisfy his hunger when he is starving. **31** Yet if he is caught, he must pay sevenfold, though it costs him all the wealth of his house. **32** But a man who commits adultery lacks judgment; whoever does so destroys himself. **33** Blows and disgrace are his lot. And his shame will never be wiped away; **34** for jealousy arouses a husband's fury, and he will show no mercy when he takes revenge. **35** He will not accept any compensation; he will refuse the bribe, however great it is.

Today's Scripture: "For these commands are a lamp, this teaching is a light, and the corrections of discipline are the way to life." (Proverbs 6:23)

Today's Wisdom: God's commands are to discipline and teach you how to succeed in life. God will never force His plans on you. He wants you to invite Him into your life so He can give you the desires of your heart.

Today's Spiritual Mindset: When you follow the commands of the Most High God, it will add many years to your life, your plans will succeed, and your future will be bright.

Spiritual Mindset Journal: It is good practice to meditate on the Word of God daily so that it will not depart from your heart. So when the enemy comes, you will open your mouth and destroy his plan with the Word that comes forth.

Use the workspace below to write verses of scripture that gave you courage when you were faced with challenges. Look for three more encouraging scriptures, write and memorize them.

_____
_____
_____
_____
_____
_____
_____
_____
_____
_____
_____
_____
_____
_____
_____
_____
_____
_____
_____
_____
_____
_____
_____
_____
_____
_____

Spiritual Mindset Action Plan: It is a good habit to begin the day praising God and meditating on His Word. When you spend time in the Word of God daily, you are feeding your body, with the exception that spiritual food is calorie-free. Unlike food, it is always tasty, with just the right seasonings. It nourishes your mind, body, and soul, and energizes you with Power from above. It is the kind of Power that no superhero can battle against. The Word of God will energize daily with the Power we need to help us overcome all the fiery darts the enemy has in store for us. Not being armed with the Word is like going out on a cold blustery day without a coat, hat, gloves, scarf, and shoes.

The Word will be all the protection that you will need when you wake up to face the day. All the crooked paths will become straight, He will detour you from danger, and His Angels will travel with you to guide and keep you during the day. When the enemy comes up against you, the Word will rise up and you will speak life into your situation and crush the enemy's head. But without the Word, you are a sitting duck, just waiting to be served as dinner. Today, make sure you reserve the first hour of your day for a power hour with God, and experience what it really means to "Have a great day."

Day Six Worksheet

1. Since you have started a daily devotion as your first activity of the day, how would you describe your attitude in general?

2. How would you describe the attitude of your family and colleagues toward you?

3. How would you describe your attitude toward your family and work associates?

_____
_____
_____
_____
_____
_____
_____
_____
_____
_____
_____
_____
_____
_____
_____
_____
_____
_____
_____
_____
_____
_____

Notes

Notes

Notes

DAY SEVEN

Today's Reading: **Proverbs Chapter 7**

My son, keep my words and store up my commands within you. **2** Keep my commands and you will live; guard my teachings as the apple of your eye. **3** Bind them on your fingers; write them on the tablet of your heart. **4** Say to wisdom, "you are my sister," and call understanding your kinsman; **5** they will keep you from the adulteress, from the wayward wife with her seductive words. **6** At the window of my house I looked out through the lattice. **7** I saw among the simple, I noticed among the young men, a youth who lacked judgment. **8** He was going down the street near her corner, walking along in the direction of her house **9** at twilight, as the day was fading, as the dark of night set in. **10** Then out came a woman to meet him, dressed like a prostitute and with crafty intent. **11** (She is loud and defiant, her feet never stay at home; **12** now in the street, now in the squares, at every corner she lurks.) **13** She took hold of him and kissed him and with a brazen face she said: **14** "I have fellowship offerings at home; today I fulfilled my vows. **15** So I came out to meet you; I looked for you and have found you! **16** I have covered my bed with colored linens from Egypt. **17** I have perfumed my bed with myrrh, aloes and cinnamon. **18** Come, let's drink deep of love till morning; let's enjoy ourselves with love! **19** My husband is not at home; he has gone on a long journey. **20** He took his purse filled with money and will not be home till full moon." **21** With persuasive words she led him astray; she seduced him with her smooth talk. **22** All at once he followed her like an ox going to the slaughter, like a deer "stepping into a noose" **23** till an arrow pierces his liver, like a bird darting into a snare, little knowing it will cost him his life.

24 Now then, my sons, listen to me; pay attention to what I say. **25** Do not let your heart turn to her ways or stray into her paths. **26** Many are the victims she has brought down; her slain are a mighty throng. **27** Her house is a highway to the grave leading down to the chambers of death.

Today's Scripture: "Guard my teachings as the apple of your eye. Bind them on your fingers; write them on the tablet of your heart." (Proverbs 2:2-3)

Today's Wisdom: When you read the scriptures and get a revelation or an "aha" moment, treasure it with all you have. Give God thanks because you have been receptive to the individualized instruction you needed that moment and for the future.

Today's Spiritual Mindset: I will hear only the voice of the Lord. I am deaf to the voice of the enemy. If I know the voice of God, I will never be misled by the voice of the enemy.

Spiritual Mindset Journal: Whose voice are you listening to? If you have the Word written on your heart, then you will not hear the persuasive words of the enemy. He will be unable to smooth talk you all the way to hell!

Use the workspace below to write those verses of scripture that your parents, Sunday school teacher, or any adult taught you as a child. If you did not receive such teachings as a child, become a parent to other children and share verses of scripture with them. Write the scripture you shared and the person with whom it was shared.

Spiritual Mindset Action Plan: Shame the devil by using your iPhone and iPad to read the Word of God and listen to music that edifies the soul. Remember, "When praises go up, Blessings come down." It's all within your reach. There's an application for that, so download your Bible app today!

With all the technology that surrounds us, it is impossible to say that we do not have access to the Word of God. The Internet can be accessed anytime, anywhere as we surf for things and places that interest us. Why not spend a few minutes each day with the only thing that will absolutely Bless and change your life forever? It is the Word of God. Even if you do not have time to open the Bible, there are many other ways to catch up with the scriptures through your phones, tablets, and computers.

Do not let unimportant, unproductive, and unfruitful things make your life so busy that you do not have any time to spend with God. As you set out today, access the Word on the radio in your car, slip in a CD with a message from your favorite ministry, or jam to your favorite gospel singer. If you travel by train, plane, or ship, pull out your smart phone, computer, or tablet and see just how spiritually smart you will be just by spending time reading or listening to the Word of God.

Day Seven Worksheet

1. Make a note of the number of times during the day when you recalled a verse of scripture, read a verse of scripture, and/or thanked God for His many Blessings.

2. You might be surprised at how much time you actually spend acknowledging God's handiwork in your life.

Notes

Notes

Notes

DAY EIGHT

Today's Reading: Proverbs Chapter 8

Does not wisdom call out? Does not understanding raise her voice? **2** On the heights along the way, where the paths meet, she takes her stand; **3** beside the gates leading into the city, at the entrances, she cried aloud: **4** "To you, O men, I call out; I raise my voice to all mankind. **5** You who are simple; gain prudence; you who are foolish, gain understanding. **6** Listen, for I have worthy things to say; I open my lips to speak what is right. **7** My mouth speaks what is true, for my lips detest wickedness. **8** All the words of my mouth are just; none of them is crooked or perverse. **9** To the discerning all of them are right; they are faultless to those who have knowledge. **10** Choose my instruction instead of silver, knowledge rather than choice gold, **11** for wisdom is more precious than rubies, and nothing you desire can compare with her. **12** "I, wisdom, dwell together with prudence; I possess knowledge and discretion. **13** To fear the Lord is to hate evil; I hate pride and arrogance, evil behavior and perverse speech. **14** Counsel and sound judgment are mine; I have understanding and power. **15** By me kings reign and rulers make laws that are just; **16** by me princes govern, and all nobles who rule on the earth. **17** I love those who love me, and those who seek me find me. **18** With me are riches and honor, enduring wealth and prosperity. **19** My fruit is better than fine gold; what I yield surpasses choice silver. **20** I walk in the way of righteousness, along the paths of justice, **21** bestowing wealth on those who love me and making their treasuries full. **22** "The Lord brought me forth as the first of his works, before his deeds of old; **23** I was appointed from eternity, from the beginning, before the world began. **24** When there were no oceans, I was given birth, when there were no springs abounding with water; **25** before the mountains were settled in place, before the hills, I was given birth, **26** before he made the earth or its fields or any of the dust of the world. **27** I was there when he set the heavens in place, when he marked out the horizon on the face of the deep, **28** when he established the clouds above and fixed securely the fountains of the deep, **29** when he gave the sea its boundary so the waters would not overstep his command, and when he marked out the foundations of the earth. **30** Then I was the craftsman at his side. I was filled with delight day after day, rejoicing always in his presence, **31** rejoicing in his whole world and delighting in mankind. **32** "Now then, my sons, listen to me; blessed are those who keep my ways. **33** Listen to my instruction and be wise; do not ignore it. **34** Blessed is the man who listens to me, watching daily at my doors, waiting at my doorway. **35** For whoever finds me finds life and receives favor from the Lord. **36** But whoever fails to find me harms himself; all who hate me love death."

Today's Scripture: "I love those who love me, and those who seek me find me." (Proverbs 8:17)

Today's Wisdom: You must love God with ALL your heart, soul, strength, and mind.

Today's Spiritual Mindset: When you fall in love with someone, they consume your mind without even trying because you make them the focus of your thoughts. Even when they hurt you or leave you, they still have access to your thoughts because you allow it.

Spiritual Mindset Journal: Fall in love with God today and let Him consume your mind, soul, and body, because He is a Love that will never leave you nor forsake you.

Use the workspace below to write reasons why you have fallen in and out of love. Ask yourself if those reasons apply to you not being in love with God. If they do not apply, find reasons to fall in love with Him.

Spiritual Mindset Action Plan: Do you know God's Love for you? He will Love you even when you disobey Him. He forgives just because you ask. His unconditional love will never be taken away from you. Sometimes in your life, you put people up on pedestals for whatever reason. It could be because you admire them, envy them, or because they make you feel good about yourself.

The danger with that obsession is that we look up to people who have just as many problems as we have, and sometimes more than we have. You admire people who are more messed up than you are. You look up to them and think that they are flawless and perfect because of their wealth, status, and popularity. In doing so, you overlook the One who created you, the One who knew you before you were born, the One who knows your deepest sorrows and greatest joys. Human beings cannot save you, because they cannot save themselves.

God will not force you to worship and serve Him or even obey His Word, because He loves you so much. He gave you free will to make the decision to serve Him. However, He is waiting for you. He is right there when you need Him. You will not be put on hold. He is accessible whenever you need Him. Just call anytime, day or night. He is truly the only Love that is worth consuming your thoughts.

Day Eight Worksheet

Write down all the gifts your First Love, God, has given you. You might start with the big things such as a planet to live on, or a small thing, such as a mustard seed. You will be surprised where you will find God.

Notes

Notes

Notes

DAY NINE

Today's Reading: Proverbs Chapter 9

Wisdom has built her house; she has hewn out its seven pillars. **2** She has prepared her meat and mixed her wine; she has also set her table. **3** She has sent out her maids, and she calls from the highest point of the city. **4** "Let all who are simple come in here!" she says to those who lack judgment. **5** "Come, eat my food and drink the wine I have mixed. **6** Leave your simple ways and you will live; walk in the way of understanding. **7** "Whoever corrects a mocker invite insult; whoever rebuke a wicked man incurs abuse. **8** Do not rebuke a mocker or he will hate you; rebuke a wise man and he will love you. **9** Instruct a wise man and he will be wiser still; teach a righteous man and he will add to his learning. **10** "The fear of the Lord is the beginning of wisdom, and knowledge of the Holy One is understanding. **11** For through me your days will be many, and years will be added to your life. **12** If you are wise, your wisdom will reward you; if you are a mocker, you alone will suffer." **13** The woman Folly is loud; she is undisciplined and without knowledge. **14** She sits at the door of her house, on a seat at the highest point of the city, **15** calling out to those who pass by, who go straight on their way. **16** "Let all who are simple come in here!" she says to those who lack judgment. **17** "Stolen water is sweet; food eaten in secret is delicious!" **18** But little do they know that the dead are there, that her guests are in the depths of the grave.

Today's Scripture: "The fear of the Lord is the beginning of Wisdom, and knowledge of the Holy One is understanding." (Proverbs 9:10)

Today's Wisdom: The book of Proverbs lets you know the wise choice of action to pursue and the foolish course of action to avoid.

Today's Spiritual Mindset: Knowing and applying the Word of God will take you off the crooked pathways to destruction, and put you on the straight and narrow path to success.

Spiritual Mindset Journal: In the spiritual realm, the opposite of ignorance is obedience, not knowledge. Are you walking in obedience that your walk and talk are in alignment with the Word of God?

Use the workspace below to write any inconsistencies you identify between your words and your actions. Write what changes you have made to have congruency. This will help to strengthen trustworthiness in you.

Spiritual Mindset Action Plan: Learning comes from experience. When you look back at your life, what are some of the mistakes you have made that cost you time, money, and/or your reputation? Did you learn anything from those mistakes? Hindsight is 20/20, but that does not change what happened. However, how can you make sure, in going forward, that your choices will not cost you more than you are willing to spend?

One of the best ways to avoid making mistakes is by learning from the mistakes of others. However, most people will never learn because they do not believe it can happen to them. Almost every day on the news, we see how bad decisions have cost people their career, family, and friends. I do not think that they set out one day to make choices that cost them everything they had worked so hard for most of their lives. Even so, I can almost guarantee that this is not the last time you will see someone involved in compromising situations at home, work, or even in the church.

The best way to avoid those life-threatening choices and situations is to make sure that your decisions and actions are in line with the Word of God. That will guarantee you will never have to apologize for what you have done! Even when the enemy tries to use a situation against you, know that God is your Defender and whatever the enemy plots for evil in your life, God will turn it around for your good. So choose wisely; make decisions that will not break your fellowship with God. What will you do differently? Today, make the decision to learn from the mistakes of others so you will not have to make them yourself. Life is too short to keep making the same mistakes.

Day Nine Worksheet

1. Do not condemn or criticize anyone for making mistakes, because you will surely experience the same or similar situation someday.

2. What mistakes have you observed others making today?

3. What corrections would you take if you were in those situations?

Notes

Notes

DAY TEN

Today's Reading: **Proverbs Chapter 10**

The proverbs of Solomon: A wise son brings joy to his father, but a foolish son grief to his mother. **2** Ill-gotten treasures are of no value, but righteousness delivers from death. **3** The Lord does not let the righteous go hungry but he thwarts the craving of the wicked. **4** Lazy hands make a man poor, but diligent hands bring wealth. **5** He who gathers crops in summer is a wise son, but he who sleeps during harvest is a disgraceful son. **6** Blessings crown the head of the righteous, but violence overwhelms the mouth of the wicked. **7** The memory of the righteous will be a blessing, but the name of the wicked will rot. **8** The wise in heart accept commands, but a chattering fool comes to ruin. **9** The man of integrity walks securely, but he who takes crooked paths will be found out. **10** He who winks maliciously causes grief, and a chattering fool comes to ruin. **11** The mouth of the righteous is a fountain of life, but violence overwhelms the mouth of the wicked. **12** Hatred stirs up dissension, but love covers over all wrongs. **13** Wisdom is found on the lips of the discerning, but a rod is for the back of him who lacks judgment. **14** Wise men store up knowledge, but the mouth of a fool invites ruin. **15** The wealth of the rich is their fortified city but poverty is the ruin of the poor. **16** the wages of the righteous bring them life, but the income of the wicked brings them punishment. **17** He who heeds discipline shows the way to life, but whosoever ignores correction leads others astray. **18** He who conceals his hatred has lying lips, and whoever spreads slander is a fool. **19** When words are many, sin is not absent, but he who holds his tongue is wise. **20** The tongue of the righteous is choice silver, but the heart of the wicked is of little value. **21** The lips of the righteous nourish many, but fools die for lack of judgment. **22** The blessing of the Lord brings wealth, and he adds no trouble to it. **23** A fool finds pleasure in evil conduct, but a man of understanding delights in wisdom. **24** What the wicked dreads will overtake him; what the righteous desire will be granted. **25** When the storm has swept by, the wicked are gone, but the righteous stand firm forever. **26** As vinegar to the teeth and smoke to the eyes, so is a sluggard to those who send him. **27** The fear of the Lord adds length to life, but the years of the wicked are cut short. **28** The prospect of the righteous is joy but the hopes of the wicked come to nothing. **29** The way of the Lord is a refuge for the righteous, but it is the ruin of those who do evil. **30** The righteous will never be uprooted, but the wicked will not remain in the land. **31** The mouth of the righteous brings forth wisdom, but a perverse tongue will be cut out. **32** The lips of the righteous know what is fitting, but the mouth of the wicked only what is perverse.

Today's Scripture: "A wise son brings joy to his father, but a foolish son grief to his mother." (Proverbs 10:1)

Today's Wisdom: Which example above best describes your relationship with your earthly parents or your Heavenly Father? If it is the latter, then repent today because those who do not, usually dies tomorrow.

Today's Spiritual Mindset: Children, obey your parents in the Lord, for this is right. "Honor your father and mother" (this is the first commandment with a promise), "that it may go well with you and that you may live long in the land. (Ephesians 6:1-3 [ESV])

Spiritual Mindset Journal: There are no new sins; we just keep recycling the old ones. Try to live a life that brings gladness and not heaviness to the Heart of God. Walk in obedience and when you stumble, all you have to do is repent.

Use the workspace below to write the things for which you are repenting. As you repent, erase and let it go into the sea of forgetfulness. Ask God for Strength and Wisdom not to make any more mistakes.

Spiritual Mindset Action Plan: There are many rules and regulations that we have to obey to maintain a civilized society. We obey the speed limit when we drive; we obey the legal age when we drink alcohol. We obey the rules on our job, in the church, and we even implement rules at home so we function well as a family. What happens when you disobey? If you go over the speed limit on the road, it can cost you some hard-earned cash or even your driving privilege. If you sell liquor to a minor, it will cost you your license or land you in jail. If you disobey your company's rules, it will eventually cost you your job. Most importantly, if you are a child who disobeys the rules of your parents, it will cost you an allowance and even get you grounded. There are rules everywhere we go, and if we disobey, there will be consequences.

God's Kingdom is no different. He has rules for us to follow in order to live long lives. When we disobey, we are bordering on life and death. Unlike some parents, who eventually give in and withhold punishment when you disobey, your heavenly Father will NEVER give in because He loves you that much. How will you ever learn the lessons that can bring death if you never receive punishment when you disobey? God wants the best for you so much that He will never reward you with something you do not deserve because there will be no lesson learned that can save your life.

Do you want to be reprimanded by God, or is it easier to just live within His guidelines? The choice is yours. Today, put wisdom to work as you make decisions based upon the Word of God. What are some of the decisions that you have to make today? List them below and see if they align with His Word.

Day Ten Worksheet

1. Do you remember a time or (times) in your life that you have broken rules and regulations.

2. What were those rules, and why was it difficult for you to follow those rules?

3. What were the consequences of breaking those rules? Was it worth it?

_____
_____
_____
_____
_____
_____
_____
_____
_____
_____
_____
_____
_____
_____
_____
_____
_____
_____
_____
_____

Notes

Notes

Notes

DAY ELEVEN

Today's Reading: Proverbs Chapter 11

The Lord abhors dishonest scales, but accurate weights are his delight. **2** When pride comes, then comes disgrace, but with humility comes wisdom. **3** The integrity of the upright guides them, but the unfaithful are destroyed by their duplicity. **4** Wealth is worthless in the day of wrath, but righteousness delivers from death. **5** The righteousness of the blameless makes a straight way for them, but the wicked are brought down by their own wickedness. **6** The righteousness of the upright delivers them, but the unfaithful are trapped by evil desires. **7** When a wicked man dies, his hope perishes; all he expected from his power comes to nothing. **8** The righteous man is rescued from trouble, and it comes on the wicked instead. **9** With his mouth the godless destroys his neighbor, but through knowledge the righteous escape. **10** When the righteous prosper, the city rejoices; when the wicked perish, there are shouts of joy. **11** Though the blessing of the upright a city is exalted, but by the mouth of the wicked it is destroyed. **12** A man who lacks judgment derides his neighbor, but a man of understanding holds his tongue. **13** A gossip betrays a confidence, but a trustworthy man keeps a secret. **14** For lack of guidance a nation falls, but many advisers make victory sure. **15** He who puts up security for another will surely suffer, but whoever refuses to strike hands in pledge is safe. **16** A kindhearted woman gains respect, but ruthless men gain only wealth. **17** A kind man benefits himself, but a cruel man brings trouble on himself. **18** The wicked man earns deceptive wages, but he who sows righteousness reaps a sure reward. **19** The truly righteous man attains life, but he who pursues evil goes to his death.

20 The Lord detests men of perverse heart but he delights in those whose ways are blameless. **21** Be sure of this: The wicked will not go unpunished, but those who are righteous will go free. **22** Like a gold ring in a pig's snout is a beautiful woman who shows no discretion. **23** The desire of the righteous ends only in good, but the hope of the wicked only in wrath. **24** One man gives freely, yet gains even more; another withholds unduly, but comes to poverty. **25** A generous man will prosper; he who refreshes others will himself be refreshed. **26** People curse the man who hoards grain, but blessing crowns him who is willing to sell. **27** He who seeks good finds goodwill, but evil comes to him who searches for it. **28** Whoever trusts in his riches will fall, but the righteous will thrive like a green leaf. **29** He who brings trouble on his family will inherit only wind, and the fool will be servant to the wise. **30** The fruit of the righteous is a tree of life, and he who win souls is wise. **31** If the righteous receive their due on earth, how much more the ungodly and the sinner!

Today's Scripture: "The fruit of the righteous is a tree of life, and he who wins souls is wise." (Proverbs 11:30)

Today's Wisdom: God wants us to be spiritual fruits, not religious nuts.

Today's Spiritual Mindset: The person who provides for this life but do not prepare for the next is wise for a moment, but a fool forever.

Spiritual Mindset Journal: I am a field worker for the Kingdom. My service is to bring in the harvest. I will not judge others because of where they are on their journey to spiritual maturity

Do you remember the first time someone shared the Gospel with you? How did you feel knowing that you have a Heavenly Father that loves you so much He gave His life to save you? How did this information change your life? How many times have you shared this amazing information with someone else who does not know his or her Heavenly Father on a personal level?

Spiritual Mindset Action Plan: As I set out today, guide my steps, O Lord, so I can be in service to whomever you bring across my path. Help me to be a friend to the friendless, a minister to the lost and broken, and an entrepreneur to those seeking entrepreneurship.

As you go about your daily lives, do you ever wonder about the people whom you meet everyday? Is it coincidence, or was it part of God's plan for you to be in contact with these individuals? Many times you ask God to Bless you, and sometimes you get upset when you do not see the Blessing manifested immediately upon request. There will be times when God will use people as a connector to you and your Blessings, as well as using you to connect people to their Blessings.

The problem is that sometimes you can become so consumed with your wants and needs that you do not observe the wants and needs of those around you. God wants you to be a Blessing wherever you go. He wants you to be aware of the people who come across your paths so you can be a Blessing to them, especially those that are assigned to you. Many times people will come across your path for ministry; sometimes they come for friendships; and other times they may cross your path because you have an opportunity to share with them.

How will you know to match a Blessing with the needs of individuals? It is simply done by asking your Heavenly Father to tell or show you the needs of others and how you can meet that need. You do not want to miss your Blessing because someone was too selfish to share it with you, even though God assigned you to that person. Similarly, you do not want to hold back on Blessing someone because you were not watching and listening when God sent that person, so you missed the opportunity to Bless him or her.

Day Eleven Worksheet

1. How many times did you miss an opportunity to Bless someone whom God sent across your path?

2. Do you remember a time when you came in contact with someone who was discouraged and you took the time to encourage or motivate him or her to continue the good fight?

3. Similarly, can you remember a stranger crossing your path and you took the time to share an opportunity with them whether it was a job, business opportunity, or just simply inviting them to church? See how many opportunities you can list below.

_____
_____
_____
_____
_____
_____
_____
_____
_____
_____
_____
_____
_____
_____
_____
_____
_____
_____

Notes

Notes

Notes

DAY TWELVE

Today's Reading: Proverbs Chapter 12

Whoever loves discipline loves knowledge, but he who hates correction is stupid. **2** A good man obtains favor from the Lord, but the Lord condemns a crafty man. **3** A man cannot be established through wickedness, but the righteous cannot be uprooted. **4** A wife of noble character is her husband's crown, but a disgraceful wife is like decay in his bones. **5** The plans of the righteous are just, but the advice of the wicked is deceitful. **6** The words of the wicked lie in wait for blood, but the speech of the upright rescues them. **7** Wicked men are overthrown and are no more, but the house of the righteous stands firm. **8** A man is praised according to his wisdom, but men with warped minds are despised. **9** Better to be a nobody and yet have a servant than pretend to be somebody and have no food. **10** A righteous man cares for the needs of his animal, but the kindest acts of the wicked are cruel. **11** He who works his land will have abundant food, but he who chases fantasies lacks judgment. **12** The wicked desire the plunder of evil men, but the root of the righteous flourishes. **13** An evil man is trapped by his sinful talk, but a righteous man escapes trouble. **14** From the fruit of his lips a man is filled with good things as surely as the work of his hands rewards him. **15** The way of a fool seems right to him, but a wise man listens to advise. **16** A fool shows his annoyance at once, but a prudent man overlooks an insult. **17** A truthful witness gives honest testimony, but a false witness tells lies. **18** Reckless words pierce like a sword, but the tongue of the wise brings healing. **19** Truthful lips endure forever but a lying tongue lasts only a moment. **20** There is deceit in the hearts of those who plot evil, but joy for those who promote peace. **21** No harm befalls the righteous, but the wicked have their fill of trouble. **22** The Lord detests lying lips, but he delights in men who are truthful. **23** A prudent man keeps his knowledge to himself, but the heart of fools blurts out folly. **24** Diligent hands will rule, but laziness ends in a slave labor. **25** An anxious heart weighs a man down, but a kind word cheers him up. **26** A righteous man is cautious in friendship, but the way of the wicked leads them astray. **27** The lazy man does not roast his game, but the diligent man prizes his possessions. **28** In the way of righteousness there is life; along that path is immortality.

Today's Scripture: "Better to be a nobody and yet have a servant than pretend to be somebody and have no food." (Proverbs 12:9)

Today's Wisdom: I will fake it only if I have established my goals and have honored my commitments to make it.

Today's Spiritual Mindset: Fear and rejection are not words that create success. They are used to describe the journey that contributed to the success.

Spiritual Mindset Journal: To be successful, I must first have a vision. "For without vision, the people perish." (Proverbs 29:18)

What does your ideal life look like? Write down everything you can think of that you want to accomplish! Keep it proactive and positive! Do not write down what you do not want; write only what you want! Think of what you want to achieve in every area of your life: Spiritual, Physical, Emotional, Relational, and Financial.

Spiritual Mindset Action Plan: Seeing is not believing, because Faith requires that I believe even when I do not see. Some of us want fame and success so badly that we are willing to do whatever it takes to get it. There are many people who, without achieving that fame or success, will pretend to have it despite the financial burden that it will cause. There are those in our society that are living above their means because they want to impress others. There are families who are in financial turmoil because they are trying to "keep up with the Joneses."

We are living in a microwave society that is pressuring us to live an illusive lifestyle because we believe that status will make us feel better about ourselves or make others like or accept us. The Bible warns us of pursuing earthly riches when we should be more concerned about storing treasures in heaven. After all, earthly treasures are temporary, and "as the world giveth, the world taketh away." The treasures that are stored up in heaven are the ones that will last forever. What do you believe for today? Do you have an unshakable faith that God is faithful to bring it to pass even when your circumstances contradict your belief?

Day Twelve Worksheet

1. Use the space below to write down the visions that God has given you for your life. It can be a talent, skill, or experience that you have been blessed with that can be a blessing to those around you.

2. How will you use your gifts to bless others?

_____
_____
_____
_____
_____
_____
_____
_____
_____
_____
_____
_____
_____
_____
_____
_____
_____
_____
_____
_____
_____
_____
_____
_____
_____
_____
_____

Notes

Notes

Notes

DAY THIRTEEN

Today's Reading: Proverbs Chapter 13

A wise son heeds his father's instruction, but a mocker does not listen to rebuke. **2** From the fruit of his lips a man enjoys good things, but the unfaithful have a craving for violence. **3** He who guards his lips guards his life, but he who speaks rashly will come to ruin. **4** The sluggard craves and gets nothing, but the desires of the diligent are fully satisfied. **5** The righteous hate what is false, but the wicked bring shame and disgrace. **6** Righteousness guards the man of integrity, but wickedness overthrows the sinner. **7** One man pretends to be rich, yet has nothing; another pretends to be poor, yet has great wealth. **8** A man's riches may ransom his life, but a poor man hears no threat. **9** The light of the righteous shines brightly, but the lamp of the wicked is snuffed out. **10** Pride only breeds quarrels, but wisdom is found in those who take advice. **11** Dishonest money dwindles away, but he who gathers money little by little makes it grow. **12** Hope deferred makes the heart sick, but a longing fulfilled is a tree of life. **13** He who scorns instruction will pay for it, but he who respects a command is rewarded. **14** The teaching of the wise is a fountain of life, turning a man from the snares of death. **15** Good understanding wins favor, but the way of the unfaithful is hard. **16** Every prudent man acts out of knowledge, but a fool exposes his folly. **17** A wicked messenger falls into trouble, but a trustworthy envoy brings healing. **18** He who ignores discipline comes to poverty and shame, but whoever heeds correction is honored. **19** A longing fulfilled is sweet to the soul, but fools detest turning from evil. **20** He who walks with the wise grows wise, but a companion of fools suffers harm. **21** Misfortune pursues the sinner, but prosperity is the reward of the righteous. **22** A good man leaves an inheritance for his children's children, but a sinner's wealth is stored up for the righteous. **23** A poor man's field may produce abundant food, but injustice sweeps it away. **24** He who spares the rod hates his son, but he who loves him is careful to discipline him. **25** The righteous eat to their hearts' content, but the stomach of the wicked goes hungry.

Today's Scripture: "He who guards his lips guards his life, but he who speaks rashly will come to ruin." (Proverbs 13:3)

Today's Spiritual Mindset: To be wise, you must seek the counsel of the wise. Keeping companion with fools will bring you to ruin.

Spiritual Mindset Journal: As life is a journey; so is success. It starts with baby steps and develops into a marathon that ends at the finish line. Until you cross that finish line, your journey continues.

When you are having a conversation with someone, do you really take the time to listen to what they are saying, or are you thinking of how you are going to respond? It has been said that the reason God gave us two ears and one mouth is because He wants us to do twice as much listening as talking.

Today, practice listening when you get into a conversation with someone. You will be amazed at how much you will learn by listening. Write down all the things that you learned because you took the time to truly listen to a friend, co-worker, or family member.

_____
_____
_____
_____
_____

Spiritual Mindset Action Plan: In the beginning, God created the earth, and one day at a time He finished His entire creation in seven days. You will not get to the top without setting goals that can be achieved one step at a time. You are not God, so do not be disappointed if you do not finish in seven days, seven months, or seven years. Sometimes, people get discouraged because they do not accomplish their plans and goals within a set period of time. Is it because God is the One who put these goals and dreams in your heart to begin with? Does He have a set time when you will achieve these goals and dreams? Of course He does, and He reveals them to you one step at a time, like breadcrumbs on a trail.

He also designed your success so it will be a Blessing to others. Before you can fulfill these goals and dreams, He wants to make sure that you can handle the responsibilities that come with them. God will not Bless you with a purpose that will eventually destroy you because you were not prepared to receive it. God has a set time for you to fulfill the goals and dreams that He put in your heart. However, the only way to become a good steward of His Blessing is to make sure that you are ready for them. He will allow you to be challenged in this life; He will allow situations that are uncomfortable and bring about changes that are unfamiliar in order to help you develop through the tests that will eventually produce your testimonies.

If you do not resist the tests and trials, they will develop you into someone who can be trusted with many gifts that will eventually be passed on to others. After all, a Blessing is not a Blessing until it is passed on to many. So in God's timing, you will receive everything He has purposed in your heart, and you will become a good steward of these gifts.

Day Thirteen Worksheet

1. What are the greatest challenges you are facing right now?

2. Challenges are designed to develop you on your journey to greatness. As you overcome the challenges, you will have a testimony to share with someone who is experiencing the same.

3. Are you prepared to hang in there, or are you going to give up and lose an opportunity for growth?

_____
_____
_____
_____
_____
_____
_____
_____
_____
_____
_____
_____
_____
_____
_____
_____
_____
_____
_____
_____
_____
_____
_____

Notes

Notes

Notes

DAY FOURTEEN

Today's Reading: **Proverbs Chapter 14**

The wise woman builds her house, but with her own hands the foolish one tears hers down. **2** He whose walk is upright fears the Lord, but he whose ways are devious despises him. **3** A fool's talk brings a rod to his back, but the lips of the wise protect them. **4** Where there are no oxen, the manger is empty, but from the strength of an ox comes an abundant harvest. **5** A truthful witness does not deceive, but a false witness pours out lies. **6** The mocker seeks wisdom and finds none, but knowledge comes easily to the discerning. **7** Stay away from a foolish man, for you will not find knowledge on his lips. **8** The wisdom of the prudent is to give thought to their ways, but the folly of fools is deception. **9** Fools mock at making amends for sin, but goodwill is found among the upright. **10** Each heart knows its own bitterness, and no one else can share its joy. **11** The house of the wicked will be destroyed, but the tent of the upright will flourish. **12** There is a way that seems right to a man, but in the end it leads to death. **13** Even in laughter the heart may ache, and joy may end in grief. **14** The faithless will be fully repaid for their ways, and the good man rewarded for his. **15** A simple man believes anything, but a prudent man gives thought to his steps. **16** A wise man fears the Lord and shuns evil, but a fool is hotheaded and reckless. **17** A quick-tempered man does foolish things, and a crafty man is hated. **18** The simple inherit folly, but the prudent are crowned with knowledge. **19** Evil men will bow down in the presence of the good, and the wicked at the gates of the righteous. **20** The poor are shunned even by their neighbors, but the rich have many friends. **21** He who despises his neighbor sins, but blessed is he who is kind to the needy. **22** Do not those who plot evil go astray? But those who plan what is good find love and faithfulness. **23** All hard work brings a profit, but mere talk leads only to poverty. **24** The wealth of the wise is their crown, but the folly of fools yields folly. **25** A truthful witness saves lives, but a false witness is deceitful. **26** He who fears the Lord has a secure fortress, and for his children it will be a refuge. **27** The fear of the Lord is a fountain of life, turning a man from the snares of death. **28** A large population is a king's glory, but without subjects a prince is ruined. **29** A patient man has great understanding, but a quick-tempered man displays folly. **30** A heart at peace gives life to the body, but envy rots the bones. **31** He who oppresses the poor shows contempt for their Maker, but whoever is kind to the needy honors God. **32** When calamity comes, the wicked are brought down, but even in death the righteous have a refuge. **33** Wisdom reposes in the heart of the discerning and even among fools she lets herself be known. **34** Righteousness exalts a nation, but sin is a disgrace to any people. **35** A king delights in a wise servant, but a shameful servant incurs his wrath.

Today's Scripture: "A large population is a king's glory, but without subjects a prince is ruined." (Proverbs 14:28)

Today's Wisdom: The journey to greatness is a lonely one if one plans to get there by oneself.

Today's Spiritual Mindset: Success achieved independently yields little reward, but success achieved in teamwork makes everyone's dream work.

Spiritual Mindset Journal: It is no fun to celebrate on the mountaintop when everyone else is stuck in the valley. True success is celebrating from the mountaintop while others are being pulled up one person at a time.

Write down in the space below some of the things you can do to help someone you know succeed. Whether you are on a job or self-employed, is there someone who is struggling in areas that you have mastered and become successful? Is there some advice that you can give them to help make their journey become just a little bit easier?

_____
_____
_____
_____
_____
_____
_____
_____
_____
_____
_____
_____
_____
_____
_____
_____
_____
_____
_____
_____
_____
_____
_____
_____
_____
_____

Spiritual Mindset Action Plan: Today I will set out to see how many people I can bless and not how many people will bless me. A successful pastor is known for his mega churches and large congregation. A successful business is made so by its vast customers and clients. A successful leader is known for the number of people that he leads. As you can see, these examples all have something in common. None of them became successful without people who contributed to that success, whether in the form or customers, clients, employees, congregation, or business partners. To make it to the top, it will take dedicated teamwork to get there.

This is just like the Kingdom, where believers play an important role in winning souls for God. Whatever role you have been called to, I am positive that in order to succeed, you must have a following to help you achieve your mission. To be an effective and successful leader on that mission, you must abandon a focus of "self-service" and adopt a focus of service to people. Whenever you are called to service and are not sure which way to go, always choose the way of serving others--and as you do so, your Heavenly Father will make sure that your needs will be taken care of in the process.

Day Fourteen Worksheet

1. How are you serving those around you? List some ways in the past week that you have been in service to others.

2. Was it in your local church, or on the job? Maybe you were serving your family.

3. Also, list some ways that you can be in service at work or at church.

Notes

Notes

Notes

DAY FIFTEEN

Today's Reading: Proverbs Chapter 15

A gentle answer turns away wrath, but a harsh word stirs up anger. **2** The tongue of the wise commends knowledge, but the mouth of the fool gushes folly. **3** The eyes of the Lord are everywhere, keeping watch on the wicked and the good. **4** The tongue that brings healing is a tree of life, but a deceitful tongue crushes the spirit. **5** A fool spurns his father's discipline, but whoever heeds correction shows prudence. **6** The house of the righteous contains great treasure, but the income of the wicked brings them trouble. **7** The lips of the wise spread knowledge; not so the hearts of fools. **8** The Lord detests the sacrifice of the wicked, but the prayer of the upright pleases him. **9** The Lord detests the way of the wicked but he loves those who pursue righteousness. **10** Stern discipline awaits him who leaves the path; he who hates correction will die. **11** Death and Destruction lie open before the Lord – how much more the hearts of men! **12** A mocker resents correction; he will not consult the wise. **13** A happy heart makes the face cheerful, but heartache crushes the spirit. **14** The discerning heart seeks knowledge, but the mouth of a fool feeds on folly. **15** All the days of the oppressed are wretched, but the cheerful heart has a continual feast. **16** Better a little with the fear of the Lord than great wealth with turmoil. **17** Better a meal of vegetables where there is love than a fattened calf with hatred. **18** A hot-tempered man stirs up dissension, but a patient man calms a quarrel. **19** The way of the sluggard is blocked with thorns, but the path of the upright is a highway. **20** A wise son brings joy to his father, but a foolish man despises his mother. **21** Folly delights a man who lacks judgment, but a man of understanding keeps a straight course. **22** Plans fail for lack of counsel, but with many advisers they succeed. **23** A man finds joy in giving an apt reply – and how good is a timely word! **24** The path of life leads upward for the wise to keep him from going down to the grave. **25** The Lord tears down the proud man's house but he keeps the widow's boundaries intact. **26** The Lord detests the thoughts of the wicked, but those of the pure are pleasing to him. **27** A greedy man brings trouble to his family, but he who hates bribes will live. **28** The heart of the righteous weighs its answers, but the mouth of the wicked gushes evil. **29** The Lord is far from the wicked but he hears the prayer of the righteous. **30** A cheerful look brings joy to the heart, and good news gives health to the bones. **31** He who listens to a life-giving rebuke will be at home among the wise. **32** He who ignores discipline despises himself, but whoever heeds correction gains understanding. **33** The fear of the Lord teaches a man wisdom, and humility comes before honor.

Today's Scripture: "A hot-tempered man stirs up dissension, but a patient man calms a quarrel." (Proverbs 15:18)

Today's Wisdom: When you master patience, you will master everything!

Today's Spiritual Mindset: I will teach others to be patient as soon as I learn to be patient myself. Some things take time. After nine months in the womb, still none of us are perfect. Unless you are Jesus, who was born perfect, you can live a lifetime and still not achieve perfection--but do not stop trying.

Spiritual Mindset Journal: Have you ever witnessed two people in an argument and neither one was willing to walk away? You stopped and listened in, and the more they argued, the less sense it made why they were involved in this heated exchange. Sometimes in life, you will have to make the decision to be the bigger person and walk away, even if the other person is at fault. Jesus teaches us to turn the other cheek, but there are times when that advice is very difficult to put into practice. Make the decision today that the next time you get involved in an argument, you will be the bigger person and walk away. If you want to have the last word, be the first one to apologize.

Think back to a time in your past when you were involved in an argument. Did it ever cross your mind that you had the power to end the argument, or was it more important to you to win the argument? Did you learn anything from that situation? Was it a fruitful exchange? If given the chance to do it again, what would you do differently? Write your thoughts below.

Spiritual Mindset Action Plan: Remember the Serenity Prayer: "God grant me the serenity to accept the things I cannot change and the patience to change the things I can." Is there anything in your life that you would like to accomplish by a certain age, but at the moment, it seems like an impossible feat? Have you talked to God about it? What did He reveal to you? Did the still small voice advise you to "wait upon the Lord," or did it say that you should take action and make it happen? It is very easy to get anxious about accomplishing things that are important to us, even if we are not being led by the Spirit to do so.

It may seem as though your victories and your breakthroughs are being delayed, but just remember that God's timing is always perfect. It may seem like others are getting their Blessings, but their timing is different from yours. God will never give your Blessing to someone else, even though it seems that there is a delay in His getting it to you. Unlike the overnight shipping services, God has never been late in making a delivery.

Day Fifteen Worksheet

1. List below the times in your life that you were waiting and believing God for a breakthrough.

2. Did you receive it?

3. Was it on time?

4. Based on your experiences, was God ever late in delivering His Blessings?

___
___
___
___
___
___
___
___
___
___
___
___
___
___
___
___
___
___
___
___
___
___
___
___

Notes

Notes

Notes

DAY SIXTEEN

Today's Reading: Proverbs Chapter 16

To man belong the plans of the heart, but from the Lord comes the reply of the tongue. **2** All a man's ways seem innocent to him, but motives are weighed by the Lord. **3** Commit to the Lord whatever you do, and your plans will succeed. **4** The Lord works out everything for his own ends – even the wicked for a day of disaster. **5** The Lord detests all the proud of heart. Be sure of this: They will not go unpunished. **6** Through love and faithfulness sin is atoned for; through the fear of the Lord a man avoids evil. **7** When a man's ways are pleasing to the Lord, he makes even his enemies live at peace with him. **8** Better a little with righteousness than much gain with injustice. **9** In his heart a man plans his course, but the Lord determines his steps. **10** The lips of a king speak as an oracle, and his mouth should not betray justice. **11** Honest scales and balances are from the Lord; all the weights in the bag are of his making. **12** Kings detest wrongdoing, for a throne is established through righteousness. **13** Kings take pleasure in honest lips; they value a man who speaks the truth. **14** A king's wrath is a messenger of death, but a wise man will appease it. **15** When a king's face brightens, it means life; his favor is like a rain cloud in spring. **16** How much better to get wisdom than gold, to choose understanding rather than silver! **17** The highway of the upright avoids evil; he who guards his way guards his life. **18** Pride goes before destruction, a haughty spirit before a fall. **19** Better to be lowly in spirit and among the oppressed than to share plunder with the proud. **20** Whoever gives heed to instruction prospers, and blessed is he who trusts in the Lord. **21** The wise in heart are called discerning, and pleasant words promote instruction. **22** Understanding is a fountain of life to those who have it, but folly brings punishment to fools. **23** A wise man's heart guides his mouth, and his lips promote instruction. **24** Pleasant words are a honeycomb, sweet to the soul and healing to the bones. **25** There is a way that seems right to a man, but in the end it leads to death. **26** The laborer's appetite works for him; his hunger drives him on. **27** A scoundrel plots evil, and his speech is like a scorching fire. **28** A perverse man stirs up dissension, and a gossip separates close friends. **29** A violent man entices his neighbor and leads him down a path that is not good. **30** He who winks with his eye is plotting perversity; he who purses his lips is bent on evil. **31** Gray hair is a crown of splendor; it is attained by a righteous life. **32** Better a patient man than a warrior, a man who controls his temper than one who takes a city. **33** The lot is cast into the lap, but its every decision is from the Lord.

Today's Scripture: "When a man's ways are pleasing to the Lord, He makes even his enemies live at peace with him." (Proverbs 16:7)

Today's Wisdom: When God writes, His pen never blots; He speaks and His tongue never slips; and when He acts, His hands will never fail.

Today's Spiritual Mindset: God is the answer regardless of what the question might be in any circumstance or situation in your life.

Spiritual Mindset Journal: God IS and always will be the Judge, Empowerer, Standard, Inspirer, Rewarder, and Author of your life. You serve an Awesome God who will not let the enemy interfere with His plans for you. God plays a role in your success, as well as you do. He has a plan for your life that is like no other. Knowing that He is in total control of your life, is there any reason why you should go through life with fears? He makes your enemies live at peace with you, so it does not matter what people do or say about you. You have a Mighty King that goes into battle for you, and He never loses.

List an instance in your life when someone was out to destroy you or your reputation. Did you turn it over to God, or did you decide to go into battle by yourself? What was the outcome? Did you lose, or did God win?

Spiritual Mindset Action Plan: God goes before you to make the crooked paths straight. He stands besides you so you do not stumble. He walks behind you so your enemies do not sneak up and overtake you. God is your shield. The enemy uses whatever he can to distract you. Did you know that the enemy is using your mean co-workers to distract and make your life unbearable? Sometimes, it is the unfriendly neighbor that complains every time a blade of grass crosses over to his property or a leaf from your tree falls on his lawn. You will not always understand the motives of people, especially when they are out seeking to destroy you without any cause.

The enemy uses them to carry out his plan to distract and discourage you into believing that God is too busy to care or protect you. He will allow the enemy to test you, but those tests will never overtake you unless you let them. Make the decision today that you will stand firm and not be moved by things that are not of God. He has promised to deliver you from the lion's mouth. He will rescue you from every evil attack, and He will bring you safely to His heavenly kingdom. To Him be the Glory forever and ever.

Day Sixteen Worksheet

1. Have you had a co-worker who would do anything to get recognized or promoted on the job, even if it meant hurting others to get to the next level?

2. Have you ever been that person?

3. List the names of those you know who allow the enemy to use them to destroy others in pursuit of success.

4. After you write down the name, say a prayer that God will turn them around and that He will use them in service to build up and not tear down those around them.

_____
_____
_____
_____
_____
_____
_____
_____
_____
_____
_____
_____
_____
_____
_____
_____

Notes

Notes

Notes

DAY SEVENTEEN

Today's Reading: **Proverbs Chapter 17**

Better a dry crust with peace and quiet than a house full of feasting, with strife. **2** A wise servant will rule over a disgraceful son, and will share the inheritance as one of the brothers. **3** The crucible for silver and the furnace for gold, but the Lord tests the heart. **4** A wicked man listens to evil lips; a liar pays attention to a malicious tongue. **5** He who mocks the poor shows contempt for their Maker; whoever gloats over disaster will not go unpunished. **6** Children's children are a crown to the aged, and parents are the pride of their children. **7** Arrogant lips are unsuited to a fool – how much worse lying lips to a ruler! **8** A bribe is a charm to the one who gives it; wherever he turns, he succeeds. **9** He who covers over an offense promotes love, but whoever repeats the matter separates close friends. **10** A rebuke impresses a man of discernment more than a hundred lashes a fool. **11** An evil man is bent only on rebellion; a merciless official will be sent against him. **12** Better to meet a bear robbed of her cubs than a fool in his folly. **13** If a man pays back evil for good, evil will never leave his house. **14** Starting a quarrel is like breaching a dam; so drop the matter before a dispute breaks out. **15** Acquitting the guilty and condemning the innocent – the Lord detests them both. **16** Of what use is money in the hand of a fool, since he has no desire to get wisdom? **17** A friend loves at all times, and a brother is born for adversity. **18** A man lacking in judgment strikes hands in pledge and puts up security for his neighbor. **19** He who loves a quarrel loves sin; he who builds a high gate invites destruction. **20** A man of perverse heart does not prosper; he whose tongue is deceitful falls into trouble. **21** To have a fool for a son brings grief; there is no joy for the father of a fool. **22** A cheerful heart is good medicine, but a crushed spirit dries up the bones. **23** A wicked man accepts a bribe in secret to pervert the course of justice. **24** A discerning man keeps wisdom in view, but a fool's eyes wander to the ends of the earth. **25** A foolish son brings grief to his father and bitterness to the one who bore him. **26** It is not good to punish an innocent man, or to flog officials for their integrity. **27** A man of knowledge uses words with restraint, and a man of understanding is even-tempered. **28** Even a fool is thought wise if he keeps silent, and discerning if he holds his tongue.

Today's Scripture: "Of what use is money in the hand of a fool, since he has no desire to get wisdom?" (Proverbs 17:16)

Today's Wisdom: When you worship God you do not make Him greater, but you are made greater when you serve Him.

Today's Spiritual Mindset: Purpose is to life as a sail to a boat. Without it, there is no course.

Spiritual Mindset Journal: Have you ever wondered why most people who win the lottery for large sums of money are usually broke within two years after receiving the windfall? Money does not buy happiness, even though it is a tough argument to win with a poor person. In our society, money, fame, and status are revered while integrity and morality are disregarded.

Can you think of someone in society in a high position who lacks integrity, but because of his or her money and status, society has overlooked their character flaws?

Spiritual Mindset Action Plan: You must always strive to live a purposeful life of service to God, because there are no trivial assignments when you work for the Lord. He makes your plans succeed when you commit them to Him. God can do more in a moment than any man can do in a millennium. He can also give you an idea or invention that will bless the lives of others as well as blessing you with financial abundance. When you wait upon the Lord and do not pursue ill-gotten gains, you will prosper in everything that you put your hands to. Ask God for wisdom in every area of your life and watch Him lead you down the paths of wealth, health, and righteousness.

Day Seventeen Worksheet

Write down some of the Blessings that you are expecting from God in each of these areas in your life: Spiritual, Physical, Financial, Relational, and Emotional.

Notes

Notes

Notes

DAY EIGHTEEN

Today's Reading: Proverbs Chapter 18

An unfriendly man pursues selfish ends; he defies all sound judgment. **2** A fool finds no pleasure in understanding but delights in airing his own opinions. **3** When wickedness comes, so does contempt, and with shame comes disgrace. **4** The words of a man's mouth are deep waters, but the fountain of wisdom is a bubbling brook. **5** It is not good to be partial to the wicked or to deprive the innocent of justice. **6** A fool's lips bring him strife, and his mouth invites a beating. **7** A fool's mouth is his undoing, and his lips are a snare to his soul. **8** The words of a gossip are like choice morsels; they go down to a man's inmost parts. **9** One who is slack in his work is brother to one who destroys. **10** The name of the Lord is a strong tower; the righteous run to it and are safe. **11** The wealth of the rich is their fortified city; they imagine it an unscalable wall. **12** Before his downfall a man's heart is proud, but humility comes before honor. **13** He who answers before listening – that is his folly and his shame. **14** A man's spirit sustains him in sickness, but a crushed spirit who can bear? **15** The heart of the discerning acquires knowledge; the ears of the wise seek it out. **16** A gift opens the way for the giver and ushers him into the presence of the great. **17** The first to present his case seems right, till another comes forward and questions him. **18** Casting the lot settles disputes and keeps strong opponents apart. **19** An offended brother is more unyielding than a fortified city, and disputes are like the barred gates of a citadel. **20** From the fruit of his mouth a man's stomach is filled; with the harvest from his lips he is satisfied. **21** The tongue has the power of life and death, and those who love it will eat its fruit. **22** He who finds a wife finds what is good and receives favor from the Lord. **23** A poor man pleads for mercy, but a rich man answers harshly. **24** A man of many companions may come to ruin, but there is a friend who sticks closer than a brother.

Today's Scripture: "The tongue has the power of life and death, and those who love it will eat its fruit." (Proverbs 18:21)

Today's Wisdom: Stick and stones may break your bones, but your tongue if not guarded, will destroy you.

Today's Spiritual Mindset: With your tongue you sing praises to God the Father, and with it you curse men who have been made in God's likeness.

Spiritual Mindset Journal: The tongue is a small part of the body, but it has the power of life and death. It can corrupt the whole body and set the course of one's life on a path to self-destruction. Your tongue can be a Blessing or a curse. It has the power to confess life or death, sickness or health, lack or prosperity. What are you confessing over your life?

Make a list below of areas in you life where you have used words to hurt and not heal. Whatever the situation, it takes as much energy to confess death as it takes to confess life. Speak to the mountains in your life and confess the Word until you see the change you are expecting in your situation.

_____
_____
_____
_____
_____
_____
_____
_____
_____
_____
_____
_____
_____
_____
_____
_____
_____
_____
_____
_____
_____
_____
_____
_____
_____
_____
_____
_____

Spiritual Mindset Action Plan: Father, help me to use my tongue today for healing rather than hurting others, no matter how much they test me. As long as I keep praising the Lord, my tongue will be very well guarded.

One of the ways to guard your tongue is to meditate on the Word of God day and night. When you study the Word of God, it has to take root in your heart. When the Word resides inside you, it will rise up and come out of your mouth at the appropriate moment. A true believer is known by his or her words and actions. The more knowledgeable you are about God, the more your thinking will come into alignment with His thoughts. Eventually, your words and actions will line up and your mind will be transformed into the mind of God.

Day Eighteen Worksheet

1. Commit some time today to get your mind and heart right with God by spending time in the Word so He can minister to the darkest corners of your heart.

2. What time of day or night will you set aside to spend time with the Creator?

3. Write a note to yourself below to remind you of your commitment to spend more time in the Word.

Notes

Notes

Notes

DAY NINETEEN

Today's Reading: Proverbs Chapter 19

Better a poor man whose walk is blameless than a fool whose lips are perverse. **2** It is not good to have zeal without knowledge, nor to be hasty and miss the way. **3** A man's own folly ruins his life, yet his heart rages against the Lord. **4** Wealth brings many friends, but a poor man's friend deserts him. **5** A false witness will not go unpunished, and he who pours out lies will not go free. **6** Many curry favor with a ruler, and everyone is the friend of a man who gives gifts. **7** A poor man is shunned by all his relatives – how much more do his friends avoid him! Though he pursues them with pleading, they are nowhere to be found. **8** He who gets wisdom loves his own soul; he who cherishes understanding prospers. **9** A false witness will not go unpunished, and he who pours out lies will perish. **10** It is not fitting for a fool to live in luxury – how much worse for a slave to rule over princes! **11** A man's wisdom gives him patience; it is to his glory to overlook an offense. **12** A king's rage is like the roar of a lion, but his favor is like dew on the grass. **13** A foolish son is his father's ruin, and a quarrelsome wife is like constant dripping. **14** Houses and wealth are inherited from parents, but a prudent wife is from the Lord. **15** Laziness brings on deep sleep, and the shiftless man goes hungry. **16** He who obeys instructions guards his life, but he who is contemptuous of his ways will die. **17** He who is kind to the poor lends to the Lord, and he will reward him for what he has done. **18** Discipline your son, for in that there is hope; do not be a willing party to his death. **19** A hot-tempered man must pay the penalty; if you rescue him, you will have to do it again. **20** Listen to advice and accept instruction, and in the end you will be wise. **21**

Many are the plans in a man's heart, but it is the Lord's purpose that prevails. **22** What a man desires is unfailing love; better to be poor than a liar. **23** The fear of the Lord leads to life: Then one rests content, untouched by trouble. **24** The sluggard buries his hand in the dish; he will not even bring it back to his mouth! **25** Flog a mocker, and the simple will learn prudence; rebuke a discerning man, and he will gain knowledge. **26** He who robs his father and drives out his mother is a son who brings shame and disgrace. **27** Stop listening to instruction, my son, and you will stray from the words of knowledge. **28** A corrupt witness mocks at justice, and the mouth of the wicked gulps down evil. **29** Penalties are prepared for mockers, and beating for the backs of fools.

Today's Scripture: "Many are the plans in a man's heart, but it is the Lord's purpose that prevails." (Proverbs 19:21)

Today's Wisdom: The pursuit of God should be the driving force for your life's purpose, inspiration, and motivation. Running from the call of God in your life will leave you bankrupt, destitute, and spiritually dead.

Today's Spiritual Mindset: The meaning of your life is not about career, money, success, or power. It is about knowing who you are in God and His plan and purpose for your life.

Spiritual Mindset Journal: The more you get to know God, the more you get to know who you are in Him. You and God are a majority. With Him ALL things are possible--but without Him, life is meaningless. God designed each one of you to play an important role in His Kingdom. What happens when you do not do your part and not live up to His plan and purpose for your life? Think of the lives that will be cheated from being blessed by you because you never received what God had in store for you or lived up to His expectation for your life.

List below what your purpose or calling is from God. In the world it is referred to as a talent. If you do not know your purpose, calling, or talent, then it is time to take it to God in prayer. List below the ways you can use your calling to win souls for The Kingdom. Are you a dancer? Will you perform a praise dance for God? Are you a singer? Will you sing songs and give praises to Him and use your voice to be a blessing to others?

_____
_____
_____
_____
_____
_____
_____
_____
_____
_____
_____
_____
_____
_____
_____
_____
_____
_____
_____
_____
_____
_____
_____
_____
_____
_____
_____
_____

Spiritual Mindset Action Plan: When your purpose becomes self-focused instead of being Christ-focused, it will bring only strife, stress, and unfulfillment into your life, career, and relationships.

Father, I commit my life and my plans into Your Hands. Let Your Will be done in every area of my life now and forevermore. Amen.

Day Nineteen Worksheet

1. Knowing that the only reason for our existence is to serve God, what are you doing in your daily life that is service-related?

2. On the lines below, write out your personal testimony of God's goodness in your life. In fact, if you are a new Believer, write a few lines of your life before knowing God, and then write the new transformation that happened after you invited Jesus into your life.

3. Share the importance of God's Word and the fact that it is the only foundation to stand on in perilous times.

_____
_____
_____
_____
_____
_____
_____
_____
_____
_____
_____
_____
_____
_____
_____
_____
_____
_____
_____

Notes

Notes

Notes

DAY TWENTY

Today's Reading: Proverbs Chapter 20

Wine is a mocker and beer a brawler; whoever is led astray by them is not wise. **2** A king's wrath is like the roar of a lion; he who angers him forfeits his life. **3** It is to a man's honor to avoid strife, but every fool is quick to quarrel. **4** A sluggard does not plow in season; so at harvest time he looks but finds nothing. **5** The purposes of a man's heart are deep waters, but a man of understanding draws them out. **6** Many a man claims to have unfailing love, but a faithful man who can find? **7** The righteous man leads a blameless life; blessed are his children after him. **8** When a king sits on his throne to judge, he winnows out all evil with his eyes. **9** Who can say, "I have kept my heart pure; I am clean and without sin"? **10** Differing weights and differing measures – the Lord detests them both. **11** Even a child is known by his actions, by whether his conduct is pure and right. **12** Ears that hear and eyes that see—the Lord has made them both. **13** Do not love sleep or you will grow poor; stay awake and you will have food to spare. **14** "It's no good, it's no good!" says the buyer; then off he goes and boasts about his purchase. **15** Gold there is, and rubies in abundance, but lips that speak knowledge are a rare jewel. **16** Take the garment of one who puts up security for a stranger; hold it in pledge if he does it for a wayward woman. **17** Food gained by fraud tastes sweet to a man, but he ends up with a mouth full of gravel. **18** Make plans by seeking advice; if you wage war, obtain guidance. **19** A gossip betrays a confidence; so avoid a man who talks too much. **20** If a man curses his father or mother, his lamp will be snuffed out in pitch darkness. **21** An inheritance quickly gained at the beginning will not be blessed at the end. **22**

Do not say, "I'll pay you back for this wrong!" Wait for the Lord, and he will deliver you. **23** The Lord detests differing weights, and dishonest scales do not please him. **24** A man's steps are directed by the Lord. How then can anyone understand his own way? **25** It is a trap for a man to dedicate something rashly and only later to consider his vows. **26** A wise king winnows out the wicked; he drives the threshing wheel over them. **27** The lamp of the Lord searches the spirit of a man; it searches out his inmost being. **28** Love and faithfulness keep a king safe; through love his throne is made secure. **29** The glory of young men is their strength, gray hair the splendor of the old. **30** Blows and wounds cleanse away evil, and beatings purge the inmost being.

Today's Scripture: "Do not love sleep or you will grow poor; stay awake and you will have food to spare." (Proverbs 20:13)

Today's Wisdom: The Bible condemns laziness, as it is an ungodly trait. The lazy and the slothful will be judged by their undoing. They will be destroyed when disaster strikes because they never bothered to prepare for it. This scripture warns that laziness and idleness always result in poverty--so love what you are doing as a vocation, and try to do your best regardless of what you are called to do. Then ask for God's Favor and Blessings in everything that you do.

Today's Spiritual Mindset: Working hard is a mindset, and so is laziness. About one-fourth of the average person's life will be spent on a job. It is essential that the Believer learn what God has to say about work so you can fulfill your responsibilities as a worker in the world and in the Kingdom.

Spiritual Mindset Journal: The sluggard is criticized because of his lazy ways. A Christ-follower does not possess the characteristics of a lazy or slothful person. God, please Bless the work of my hands today. Let me do my work as unto You, Lord, so everything I touch turns to solid gold.

List all the projects or assignments that you have pending. Ask God what you want Him to help you accomplish in finalizing your work. If you do not have pending or ongoing projects, ask God to give you witty ideas and inventions, and start listening to His still small voice as it begins to direct your path to success.

_____
_____
_____
_____
_____
_____
_____
_____
_____
_____
_____
_____
_____
_____
_____
_____
_____
_____
_____
_____
_____
_____
_____
_____

Spiritual Mindset Action Plan: Ask God to bring you opportunities that will help you become a hard worker in everything you do. Then look for His answer in every area of your life (work, home, school, ministry).

Day Twenty Worksheet

1. To abandon laziness and pursue excellence means that the Holy Spirit must control you. In order to overcome laziness, ask the Spirit to make you a hard worker for God.

2. Meditate on the scriptures in Proverbs that pertains to laziness.

3. Ask God to help you overcome any bad habits that have contributed to your laziness.

4. When you are tempted to be lazy, pray and ask the Spirit to guide you and remind you of what the Father says about laziness.

5. Make sure you journal your experiences so when you look back to this day, you will see how productive you have become.

Notes

Notes

Day Twenty-One

Today's Reading: **Proverbs Chapter 21**

The king's heart is in the hand of the Lord; he directs it like a watercourse wherever he pleases. **2** All a man's ways seem right to him, but the Lord weighs the heart. **3** To do what is right and just is more acceptable to the Lord than sacrifice. **4** Haughty eyes and a proud heart, the lamp of the wicked, are sin! **5** The plans of the diligent lead to profit as surely as haste leads to poverty. **6** A fortune made by a lying tongue is a fleeting vapor and a deadly snare. **7** The violence of the wicked will drag them away, for they refuse to do what is right. **8** The way of the guilty is devious, but the conduct of the innocent is upright. **9** Better to live on a corner of the roof than share a house with a quarrelsome wife. **10** The wicked man craves evil; his neighbor gets no mercy from him. **11** When a mocker is punished, the simple gain wisdom; when a wise man is instructed, he gets knowledge. **12** The Righteous One takes note of the house of the wicked and brings the wicked to ruin. **13** If a man shuts his ears to the cry of the poor, he too will cry out and not be answered. **14** A gift given in secret soothes anger, and a bribe concealed in the cloak pacifies great wrath. **15** When justice is done, it brings joy to the righteous but terror to evildoers. **16** A man who strays from the path of understanding comes to rest in the company of the dead. **17** He who loves pleasure will become poor; whoever loves wine and oil will never be rich. **18** The wicked becomes a ransom for the righteous, and the unfaithful for the upright. **19** Better to live in a desert than with a quarrelsome and ill-tempered wife. **20** In the house of the wise are stores of choice food and oil, but a foolish man devours all he has. **21** He who pursues righteousness and love finds life, prosperity and honor. **22** A wise man attacks the city of the mighty and pulls down the stronghold in which they trust. **23** He who guards his mouth and his tongue keeps himself from calamity. **24** The proud and arrogant man –"Mocker" is his name; he behaves with overweening pride. **25** The sluggard's craving will be the death of him, because his hands refuse to work. **26** All day long he craves for more, but the righteous give without sparing. **27** The sacrifice of the wicked is detestable – how much more so when brought with evil intent! **28** A false witness will perish, and whoever listens to him will be destroyed forever. **29** A wicked man puts up a bold front, but an upright man gives thought to his ways. **30** There is no wisdom, no insight, no plan that can succeed against the Lord. **31** The horse is made ready for the day of battle, but victory rests with the Lord.

Today's Scripture: "The horse is made ready for the day of battle, but victory rests with the Lord." (Proverbs 21:31)

Today's Wisdom: The Lord is the author and finisher of our faith.

Today's Spiritual Mindset: Before the use of technology to perfect military weapons, the horse was used primarily for battle. Horses were prepared and trained to go into battle, and men put great confidence in the performance of their horses. The horse was a vain means of victory.

Spiritual Mindset Journal: No matter how prepared you are for the challenges and circumstance brought about by the enemy, it is God who delivers the final victory. Safety can be found only in the Lord, because He is the Only One that can deliver you in every battle.

List three (3) separate times below when you were in battle, and God took over and turned the situation around and gave you complete victory over the enemy.

_____
_____
_____
_____
_____
_____
_____
_____
_____
_____
_____
_____
_____
_____
_____
_____
_____
_____
_____
_____
_____
_____
_____
_____
_____

Spiritual Mindset Action Plan: Father, as I go about my day, help me to be Victorious in every situation the enemy brings my way. I know that I have already won, so I thank You in advance for the power to win.

Day Twenty-One Worksheet

1. On the lines below, list some of your vain means of victory. In other words, what are some of the things that you have unintentionally put above God as a means of security?

2. Was it the security of a job, the safety net of a bank account, or the protection of your home security system?

3. Did this false sense of security provide adequate protection when you went to battle with the enemy?

4. There is Only One sure guarantee of protection in life, and it is to know that God has and will ALWAYS protect His children in every situation!

_____
_____
_____
_____
_____
_____
_____
_____
_____
_____
_____
_____
_____
_____
_____
_____
_____

Notes

Notes

DAY TWENTY-TWO

Today's Reading: Proverbs Chapter 22

A good name is more desirable than great riches; to be esteemed is better than silver or gold. **2** Rich and poor have this in common: The Lord is the Maker of them all. **3** A prudent man sees danger and takes refuge, but the simple keep going and suffer for it. **4** Humility and the fear of the Lord bring wealth and honor and life. **5** In the paths of the wicked lie thorns and snares, but he who guards his soul stays far from them. **6** Train a child in the way he should go, and when he is old he will not turn from it. **7** The rich rule over the poor, and the borrower is servant to the lender. **8** He who sows wickedness reaps trouble, and the rod of his fury will be destroyed. **9** A generous man will himself be blessed, for he shares his food with the poor. **10** Drive out the mocker, and out goes strife; quarrels and insults are ended. **11** He who loves a pure heart and whose speech is gracious will have the king for his friend. **12** The eyes of the Lord keep watch over knowledge, but he frustrates the words of the unfaithful. **13** The sluggard says, "There is a lion outside!" or, "I will be murdered in the streets!" **14** The mouth of an adulteress is a deep pit; he who is under the Lord's wrath will fall into it. **15** Folly is bound up in the heart of a child, but the rod of discipline will drive it far from him. **16** He who oppresses the poor to increase his wealth and he who gives gifts to the rich – both come to poverty. **17** Pay attention and listen to the sayings of the wise; apply your heart to what I teach, **18** for it is pleasing when you keep them in your heart and have all of them ready on your lips. **19** So that your trust may be in the Lord, I teach you today, even you. **20** Have I not written thirty sayings for you, sayings of counsel and knowledge,

21 teaching you true and reliable words, so that you can give sound answers to him who sent you? **22** Do not exploit the poor because they are poor and do not crush the needy in court, **23** for the Lord will take up their case and will plunder those who plunder them. **24** Do not make friends with a hot-tempered man, do not associate with one easily angered, **25** or you may learn his ways and get yourself ensnared. **26** Do not be a man who strikes hands in pledge or puts up security for debts; **27** if you lack the means to pay, your very bed will be snatched from under you. **28** Do not move an ancient boundary stone set up by your forefathers. **29** Do you see a man skilled in his work? He will serve before kings; he will not serve before obscure men.

Today's Scripture: "The rich rule over the poor, and the borrower is servant to the lender." (Proverbs 22:7)

Today's Wisdom: For it is "the Lord who gives us the Power to produce wealth." (Deut. 8:18) When we pursue riches and fame outside of the Kingdom, we risk becoming slaves in the pursuit of material things.

Today's Spiritual Mindset: True Wealth comes from God, and He will add no sorrow to it. The world crowns fame and success, but God Honors Holiness.

Spiritual Mindset Journal: Do not wait for God to remind you that He is the source of everything you have. Always remember that any success that costs you the Blessing of the Lord is success you simply cannot afford. Ask God to help you to live within your means so you can be a lender to many and a borrower to none.

Can you remember a time when you pursued something even though you knew that it was not in line with the Word of God for your life? (e.g. pursue a relationship, apply for a job, make a purchase, invest in a business). What did your disobedience cost you?

_____
_____
_____
_____
_____
_____
_____
_____
_____
_____
_____
_____
_____
_____
_____
_____
_____
_____
_____
_____
_____
_____
_____
_____
_____
_____
_____
_____
_____

Spiritual Mindset Action Plan: A borrower gives up some control and freedom over his life to his lender. In other words, when you are in debt, it is difficult to have peace of mind. You are not free to live life unlimited because your debt is limiting you from the things that God has called you to do. For example, you might have to work multiple jobs just to pay off amassed debt, leaving no time for family and friends, or to fellowship with your brothers and sisters in Christ. You may not be able to go on a vacation because you have to work overtime to get caught up on your bills. This is the relationship that the slave has with his master. The slave is not free to live the life that God has created him to live.

Day Twenty-Two Worksheet

1. What is your relationship with your lenders or creditors?

2. Is it a relationship where each of you is a Blessing to the other, or is it a form of New Age slavery? For example, maybe you have used up all of your vacation or sick time at work and were advanced days that you now have to pay back. You have to continue working with no time for rest because you owe your employer time. Maybe it is your credit card debts that have you working for the next 100 years only to pay off the interest, so retirement is not an option.

3. Write on the lines below the area of your life where you are in debt to a lender. Then write out a plan for what has to be done in order to take back control of your freedom, your finances, and your life.

_____
_____
_____
_____
_____
_____
_____
_____
_____
_____
_____
_____
_____
_____
_____
_____

Notes

Notes

Notes

DAY TWENTY-THREE

―⚬⚬⚬―

Today's Reading: Proverbs Chapter 23

When you sit to dine with a ruler, note well what is before you, **2** and put a knife to your throat if you are given to gluttony. **3** Do not crave his delicacies, for that food is deceptive. **4** Do not wear yourself out to get rich; have the wisdom to show restraint. **5** Cast but a glance at riches, and they are gone, for they will surely sprout wings and fly off to the sky like an eagle. **6** Do not eat the food of a stingy man, do not crave his delicacies; **7** for he is the kind of man who is always thinking about the cost. "Eat and drink," he says to you, but his heart is not with you. **8** You will vomit up the little you have eaten and will have wasted your compliments. **9** Do not speak to a fool, for he will scorn the wisdom of your words. **10** Do not move an ancient boundary stone or encroach on the fields of the fatherless, **11** for their Defender is strong; he will take up their case against you. **12** Apply your heart to instruction and your ears to words of knowledge. **13** Do not withhold discipline from a child; if you punish him with the rod, he will not die. **14** Punish him with the rod and save his soul from death. **15** My son, if your heart is wise, then my heart will be glad; **16** my inmost being will rejoice when your lips speak what is right. **17** Do not let your heart envy sinners, but always be zealous for the fear of the Lord. **18** There is surely a future hope for you, and your hope will not be cut off. **19** Listen, my son, and be wise, and keep your heart on the right path. **20** Do not join those who drink too much wine or gorge themselves on meat, **21** for drunkards and gluttons become poor, and drowsiness clothes them in rags. **22** Listen to your father, who gave you life, and do not despise your mother when she is old. **23** Buy the truth and do not sell it; get wisdom, discipline and understanding. **24** The father of a righteous man has great joy; he who has a wise son delights in him. **25** May your father and mother be glad; may she who gave you birth rejoice! **26** My son, give me your heart and let your eyes keep to my ways, **27** for a prostitute is a deep pit and a wayward wife is a narrow well. **28** Like a bandit she lies in wait, and multiplies the unfaithful among men. **29** Who has woe? Who has sorrow? Who has strife? Who has complaints? Who has needless bruises? Who has bloodshot eyes? **30** Those who linger over wine, who go to sample bowls of mixed wine. **31** Do not gaze at wine when it is red, when it sparkles in the cup, when it goes down smoothly! **32** In the end it bites like a snake and poisons like a viper. **33** Your eyes will see strange sights and your mind imagine confusing things. **34** You will be like one sleeping on the high seas, lying on top of the rigging. **35** "They hit me," you will say, "but I'm not hurt! They beat me, but I don't feel it! When will I wake up so I can find another drink?"

Today's Scripture: "Buy the truth and do not sell it; get wisdom, discipline and understanding." (Proverbs 23:23)

Today's Wisdom: "And ye shall know the truth, and the truth shall make you free." (John 8:32)

Today's Spiritual Mindset: It is always easier to tell the truth, because keeping up with a lie is very hard work. There is no such thing as a little white lie. The Bible condemns a lying and deceitful person. A lying tongue brings destruction upon its victim--so choose to utter the life-giving Word of God.

Spiritual Mindset Journal: The truth always keeps you on a straight and narrow path, but error will take you in all directions. God does not want us to have a divided heart between Him and the world. He wants ALL or nothing.

When was the last time you told a lie? Did it hurt you or someone else? Make a list below, and maybe it is time to make things right.

Spiritual Mindset Action Plan: In the scripture the word "Truth" is referring to Jesus Christ the Way and the Life that was bought for us through the shedding of His precious blood. The other Truth is referring to thing that has been entrusted, revealed, or gifted to us that is beneficial to Blessing others and promoting God's Love.

Day Twenty-Three Worksheet

1. In the spaces below, write down some of the truths that you believe are from Him and have been entrusted to you to share or give to others so they can do the same for God's glory.

2. Remember, the system of the world is buying and selling (for profit). In God's system, it is giving/sharing for the glory of God.

_____
_____
_____
_____
_____
_____
_____
_____
_____
_____
_____
_____
_____
_____
_____
_____
_____
_____
_____
_____
_____
_____
_____
_____
_____

Notes

Notes

Notes

DAY TWENTY-FOUR

Today's Reading: Proverbs Chapter 24

Do not envy wicked men, do not desire their company; **2** for their hearts plot violence, and their lips talk about making trouble. **3** By wisdom a house is built, and through understanding it is established; **4** through knowledge its rooms are filled with rare and beautiful treasures. **5** A wise man has great power, and a man of knowledge increases strength; **6** for waging war you need guidance, and for victory many advisers. **7** Wisdom is too high for a fool; in the assembly at the gate he has nothing to say. **8** He who plots evil will be known as a schemer. **9** The schemes of folly are sin, and men detest a mocker. **10** If you falter in times of trouble, how small is your strength! **11** Rescue those being led away to death; hold back those staggering toward slaughter. **12** If you say, "But we knew nothing about this," does not he who weighs the heart perceive it? Does not he who guards your life know it? Will he not repay each person according to what he has done? **13** Eat honey, my son, for it is good; honey from the comb is sweet to your taste. **14** Know also that wisdom is sweet to your soul; if you find it, there is a future hope for you, and your hope will not be cut off. **15** Do not lie in wait like an outlaw against a righteous man's house, do not raid his dwelling place; **16** for though a righteous man falls seven times, he rises again, but the wicked are brought down by calamity. **17** Do not gloat when your enemy falls; when he stumbles, do not let your heart rejoice, **18** or the Lord will see and disapprove and turn his wrath away from him. **19** Do not fret because of evil men or be envious of the wicked, **20** for the evil man has no future hope, and the lamp of the wicked will be snuffed out. **21** Fear the Lord and the king, my son, and do not join with the rebellious, **22** for those two will send sudden destruction upon them, and who knows what calamities they can bring? **23** These also are sayings of the wise: To show partiality in judging is not good: **24** Whoever says to the guilty, "You are innocent"- peoples will curse him and nations denounce him. **25** But it will go well with those who convict the guilty, and rich blessing will come upon them. **26** An honest answer is like a kiss on the lips. **27** Finish your outdoor work and get your fields ready; after that, build your house. **28** Do not testify against your neighbor without cause, or use your lips to deceive. **29** Do not say, "I'll do to him as he has done to me; I'll pay that man back for what he did." **30** I went past the field of the sluggard, past the vineyard of the man who lacks judgment; **31** thorns had come up everywhere, the ground was covered with weeds, and the stone wall was in ruins. **32** I applied my heart to what I observed and learned a lesson from what I saw: **33** A little sleep, a little slumber, a little folding of the hands to rest **–34** and poverty will come on you like a bandit and scarcity like an armed man.

Today's Scripture: "If you falter in times of trouble, how small is your strength!" (Proverbs 24:10)

Today's Wisdom: "The name of the Lord is a fortified tower; the righteous run to it and are safe." (Proverbs 18:10)

Today's Spiritual Mindset: The Victory is not in the easy tests, but in the life-threatening, life-altering, and life-challenging struggles along the way.

Spiritual Mindset Journal: Do not despise the mountains in your life. God is using them to develop and perfect you for His Glory. The climb is necessary to get to the top, so do not be distracted by the surroundings; do not look down in the valley. Just keep climbing!

Make a list below of the mountains that are in your life right now. Then spend a few minutes asking God to strengthen you and reveal to you the lessons that will help you overcome.

_____
_____
_____
_____
_____
_____
_____
_____
_____
_____
_____
_____
_____
_____
_____
_____
_____
_____
_____
_____
_____
_____
_____
_____
_____

Spiritual Mindset Action Plan: In times of trouble, do you call upon the Lord or your friends? Though your strength is small, greater is the strength of the One who lives within you. What do you do in times of trial? Do you endeavor to be doubly courageous, or does your strength amount to nothing?

Day Twenty-Four Worksheet

1. When I think of strength, I think of the tiny plants that have caused pavements to crack and crumble because of the force that was exerted while growing and becoming massive trees. In times of trouble, how do you react? Do you cry, whine, panic--or do you have a pity party and complain to those around you?

2. The next time you are faced with trials and challenges, seek the Lord for the power and endurance you need to quietly and cheerfully face your situation. Solomon has continually encouraged us to internalize the wisdom that will help us overcome adversity. Nehemiah 8:10 tells us "the joy of the Lord is your strength." Paul says in Ephesians 6:10 "Be strong in the Lord and in the power of his might."

3. How strong are you? Think about it and list below your new-found strength to overcome in times of trouble.

Notes

Notes

DAY TWENTY-FIVE

Today's Reading: Proverbs Chapter 25

These are more proverbs of Solomon, copied by the men of Hezekiah king of Judah: **2** It is the glory of God to conceal a matter; to search out a matter is the glory of kings. **3** As the heavens are high and the earth is deep, so the hearts of kings are unsearchable. **4** Remove the dross from the silver, and out comes material for the silversmith; **5** remove the wicked from the king's presence, and his throne will be established through righteousness. **6** Do not exalt yourself in the king's presence, and do not claim a place among great men; **7** it is better for him to say to you, "Come up here," than for him to humiliate you before a nobleman. What you have seen with your eyes **8** do not bring hastily to court, for what will you do in the end if your neighbor puts you to shame? **9** If you argue your case with a neighbor, do not betray another man's confidence, **10** or he who hears it may shame you and you will never lose your bad reputation. **11** A word aptly spoken is like apples of gold in settings of silver. **12** Like an earring of gold or an ornament of fine gold is a wise man's rebuke to a listening ear. **13** Like the coolness of snow at harvest time is a trustworthy messenger to those who send him; he refreshes the spirit of his masters. **14** Like clouds and wind without rain is a man who boasts of gifts he does not give. **15** Through patience a ruler can be persuaded, and a gentle tongue can break a bone. **16** If you find honey, eat just enough – too much of it, and you will vomit. **17** Seldom set foot in your neighbor's house – too much of you, and he will hate you. **18** Like a club or a sword or a sharp arrow is the man who gives false testimony against his neighbor. **19** Like a bad tooth or a lame foot is reliance on the unfaithful in times of trouble. **20** Like one who takes away a garment on a cold day, or like vinegar poured on soda, is one who sings songs to a heavy heart. **21** If your enemy is hungry, give him food to eat; if he is thirsty, give him water to drink. **22** In doing this, you will heap burning coals on his head, and the Lord will reward you. **23** As a north wind brings rain, so a sly tongue brings angry looks. **24** Better to live on a corner of the roof than share a house with a quarrelsome wife. **25** Like cold water to a weary soul is good news from a distant land. **26** Like a muddied spring or a polluted well is a righteous man who gives way to the wicked. **27** It is not good to eat too much honey, nor is it honorable to seek one's own honor. **28** Like a city whose walls are broken down is a man who lacks self-control.

Scripture Reading: "Like an earring of gold or an ornament of fine gold is a wise man's rebuke to a listening ear." (Proverbs 25:12)

Today's Wisdom: A good leader is called to be a wise rebuker.

Today's Spiritual Mindset: A wise rebuker is willing to give rebuke or warning when it is required, and speaks it with grace, truth, and love.

Spiritual Mindset Journal: An obedient ear is required to receive rebuke. A person willing to receive it without offense because of pride or shame will walk in knowledge and increase in strength.

List three (3) instances below when you disobeyed authority or someone disobeyed your authority.

_____

Spiritual Mindset Action Plan: O Lord, help me to give rebuke with grace, truth, and love. Help me to receive it with an obedient ear, and give me wisdom to resist when it contradicts your Word.

Day Twenty-Five Worksheet

1. The interpretation of the verse can be explained that by standing together as golden earrings are coordinated with a golden necklace, a beautiful and mutual relationship is formed. The same can be said for a wise speaker and a hearer who listens to his admonitions.

2. List below a time in your past that you were rebuked, but the pain was lessened because of the person who rebuked you. Did you heed his or her words?

3. How did it contribute to your growth and development?

_____
_____
_____
_____
_____
_____
_____
_____
_____
_____
_____
_____
_____
_____
_____
_____
_____
_____
_____

Notes

Notes

DAY TWENTY-SIX

Today's Reading: Proverbs Chapter 26

Like snow in summer or rain in harvest, honor is not fitting for a fool. **2** Like a fluttering sparrow or a darting swallow, an undeserved curse does not come to rest. **3** A whip for the horse, a halter for the donkey, and a rod for the backs of fools! **4** Do not answer a fool according to his folly, or you will be like him yourself. **5** Answer a fool according to his folly, or he will be wise in his own eyes. **6** Like cutting off one's feet or drinking violence is the sending of a message by the hand of a fool. **7** Like a lame man's legs that hang limp is a proverb in the mouth of a fool. **8** Like tying a stone in a sling is the giving of honor to a fool. **9** Like a thornbush in a drunkard's hand is a proverb in the mouth of a fool. **10** Like an archer who wounds at random is he who hires a fool or any passer-by. **11** As a dog returns to its vomit, so a fool repeats his folly. **12** Do you see a man wise in his own eyes? There is more hope for a fool than for him. **13** The sluggard says, "There is a lion in the road, a fierce lion roaming the streets!" **14** As a door turns on its hinges, so a sluggard turns on his bed. **15** The sluggard buries his hand in the dish; he is too lazy to bring it back to his mouth. **16** The sluggard is wiser in his own eyes that seven men who answer discreetly. **17** Like one who seizes a dog by the ears is a passer-by who meddles in a quarrel not his own. **18** Like a madman shooting firebrands or deadly arrows **19** is a man who deceives his neighbor and says, "I was only joking!" **20** Without wood a fire goes out; without gossip a quarrel dies down. **21** As charcoal to embers and as wood to fire, so is a quarrelsome man for kindling strife. **22** The words of a gossip are like choice morsels; they go down to a man's inmost parts. **23** like a coating of glaze over earthenware are fervent lips with an evil heart. **24** A malicious man disguises himself with his lips, but in his heart he harbors deceit. **25** Though his speech is charming, do not believe him, for seven abominations fill his heart. **26** His malice may be concealed by deception, but his wickedness will be exposed in the assembly. **27** If a man digs a pit, he will fall into it, if a man rolls a stone, it will roll back on him. **28** A lying tongue hates those it hurts, and a flattering mouth works ruin.

Today's Scripture: "Without wood a fire goes out; without gossip a quarrel dies down." (Proverbs 26:20)

Today's Wisdom: Gentle words extinguish a quarrel, but a harsh word ignites a fight.

Today's Spiritual Mindset: Today's story is yesterday's news, whether it is true or not. If you do not talk about it and spread rumors, a fight or argument will stop.

Spiritual Mindset Journal: You must stop gossiping or you will be on the receiving end of an argument or fight.

List three (3) times you were the subject of a gossip in your neighborhood, church, or on the job. How did it make you feel to be on the receiving end?

_____
_____
_____
_____
_____
_____
_____

Spiritual Mindset Action Plan: In order to keep a fire going, you have to keep adding wood. When the last ember is gone, so is the fire. Slander cannot be propagated if it is not received. The tale-bearer and the tale-receiver are the agents of discord. Hence the proverbs "The receiver is as bad as the thief." The law treats them equally. The one who receives stolen goods, knowing that they are stolen, will be hanged, as well as the one who stole them.

Day Twenty-Six Worksheet

1. Now list three (3) situations when you were an agent of gossip. Have you ever purchased discounted goods with the knowledge that they were stolen?

2. You cannot change the past, so now that you know it was wrong, it is time to ask God to forgive you as you embark on your journey to greatness.

Notes

Notes

Day Twenty-Seven

Today's Reading: Proverbs Chapter 27

Do not boast about tomorrow, for you do not know what a day may bring forth. **2** Let another praise you, and not your own mouth; someone else, and not your own lips. **3** Stone is heavy and sand a burden, but provocation by a fool is heavier than both. **4** Anger is cruel and fury overwhelming, but who can stand before jealousy? **5** Better is open rebuke than hidden love. **6** Wounds from a friend can be trusted, but an enemy multiplies kisses. **7** He who is full loathes honey, but to the hungry even what is bitter tastes sweet. **8** Like a bird that strays from its nest is a man who strays from his home. **9** Perfume and incense bring joy to the heart, and the pleasantness of one's friend springs from his earnest counsel. **10** Do not forsake your friend and the friend of your father, and do not go to your brother's house when disaster strikes you – better a neighbor nearby than a brother far away. **11** Be wise, my son, and bring joy to my heart; then I can answer anyone who treats me with contempt. **12** The prudent see danger and take refuge, but the simple keep going and suffer for it. **13** Take the garment of one who puts up security for a stranger; hold it in pledge if he does it for a wayward woman. **14** If a man loudly blesses his neighbor early in the morning, it will be taken as a curse. **15** A quarrelsome wife is like a constant dripping on a rainy day; **16** restraining her is like restraining the wind or grasping oil with the hand. **17** As iron sharpens iron, so one man sharpens another. **18** He who tends a fig tree will eat its fruit, and he who looks after his master will be honored. **19** As water reflects a face, so a man's heart reflects the man. **20** Death and destruction are never satisfied, and neither are the eyes of man. **21** The crucible for silver and the furnace for gold, but man is tested by the praise he receives. **22** Though you grind a fool in a mortar, grinding him like grain with a pestle, you will not remove his folly from him. **23** Be sure you know the condition of your flocks, give careful attention to your herds; **24** for riches do not endure forever, and a crown is not secure for all generations. **25** When the hay is removed and new growth appears and the grass from the hills is gathered in, **26** the lambs will provide you with clothing, and the goats with the price of a field. **27** You will have plenty of goats' milk to feed you and your family and to nourish your servant girls.

Today's Scripture: "As iron sharpens iron, so one man sharpens another." (Proverbs 27:17)

Today's Wisdom: A man's spiritual mind sharpens the mind of his friend spiritually.

Today's Spiritual Mindset: We are our brother's keeper and are responsible to do so in a godly manner with love, trust, and honesty.

Spiritual Mindset Journal: As we surrender our lives to God and let Him develop us into whom He created us to be, we can impact the lives of others when we show them how to live for Him only.

List a time when someone impacted your life and you knew without a shadow of a doubt that they were sent by God.

_____
_____
_____
_____
_____
_____
_____

Spiritual Mindset Action Plan: Father, let my light shine before men. Let me be a living example of Your Kingdom. Let my walk and talk align with your Word, and let my light illuminate the darkness of the evil one.

Day Twenty-Seven Worksheet

1. For as long as you can remember, name a few instances when you were able to bless others based on what you learned from the Word of God. For example, did you invest some time to train and develop them in a particular field?

2. Did you purchase developmental tools to help them grow and develop an area of their life (spiritually, financially, relationally, physically, or emotionally)?

3. Did you bring them to church with you so the Holy Spirit could minister to their heart?

4. List some or all of your experiences in those areas. If you cannot think of any, maybe its time to start being a blessing to others and experiencing the joy it brings.

Notes

Notes

Day Twenty-Eight

Today's Reading: Proverbs Chapter 28

The wicked man flees though no one pursues, but the righteous are as bold as a lion. **2** When a country is rebellious, it has many rulers, but a man of understanding and knowledge maintains order. **3** A ruler who oppresses the poor is like a driving rain that leaves no crops. **4** Those who forsake the law praise the wicked, but those who keep the law resist them. **5** Evil men do not understand justice, but those who seek the Lord understand it fully. **6** Better a poor man whose walk is blameless than a rich man whose ways are perverse. **7** He who keeps the law is a discerning son, but a companion of gluttons disgraces his father. **8** He who increases his wealth by exorbitant interest amasses it for another, who will be kind to the poor. **9** If anyone turns a deaf ear to the law, even his prayers are detestable. **10** He who leads the upright along an evil path will fall into his own trap, but the blameless will receive a good inheritance. **11** A rich man may be wise in his own eyes, but a poor man who has discernment sees through him. **12** When the righteous triumph, there is great elation; but when the wicked rise to power, men go into hiding. **13** He who conceals his sins does not prosper, but whoever confesses and renounces them finds mercy. **14** Blessed is the man who always fears the Lord, but he who hardens his heart falls into trouble. **15** Like a roaring lion or a charging bear is a wicked man ruling over a helpless people. **16** A tyrannical ruler lacks judgment, but he who hates ill-gotten gain will enjoy a long life. **17** A man tormented by the guilt of murder will be a fugitive till death; let no one support him. **18** He whose walk is blameless is kept safe, but he whose ways are perverse will suddenly fall. **19** He who works his land will have abundant food, but the one who chases fantasies will have his fill of poverty. **20** A faithful man will be richly blessed, but one eager to get rich will not go unpunished. **21** To show partiality is not good – yet a man will do wrong for a piece of bread. **22** A stingy man is eager to get rich and is unaware that poverty awaits him. **23** He who rebukes a man will in the end gain more favor than he who has a flattering tongue. **24** He who robs his father or mother and says, "It's not wrong" – he is partner to him who destroys. **25** A greedy man stirs up dissension, but he who trusts in the Lord will prosper **26** He who trust in himself is a fool, but he who walks in wisdom is kept safe. **27** He who gives to the poor will lack nothing, but he who closes his eyes to them receives many curses. **28** When the wicked rise to power, people go into hiding; but when the wicked perish, the righteous thrive.

Today's Scripture: "A greedy man stirs up dissension, but he who trusts in himself is a fool, but he who walks in wisdom is kept safe." (Proverbs 28:25)

Today's Wisdom: God's plan and purpose are to make something beautiful out of the raw material of your life; you can choose the life of the wise or the life of a fool; the choice is yours!

Today's Spiritual Mindset: A truly wise person asks God for Wisdom and it shall cost him nothing.

Spiritual Mindset Journal: You can be wise with an IQ of 60 or you can be a fool with an IQ of 160. What is your spiritual IQ? If you cannot answer this question, then it's time to dig into the Word of God and let Him develop you in His Word, starting from the inside out. In the end, it is all that matters.

List a few of the ways you can begin to develop your spiritual IQ, meaning your knowledge of the Word. Here is a hint (daily Bible

reading and meditation). **How can you use the knowledge to help you advance God's Kingdom?**

_____
_____
_____
_____
_____
_____
_____
_____
_____
_____
_____
_____
_____
_____
_____
_____
_____
_____
_____
_____
_____
_____
_____
_____
_____

Spiritual Mindset Action Plan: The only way you will lack Wisdom is if you have not asked. God tells us in His Word to ask for Wisdom and understanding, because He gives it for free.

Day Twenty-Eight Worksheet

1. Do you seek God's help when you make important decisions in your life, or do you make them and hope to God they work out in your favor? You do not have to play Russian roulette when it comes to making the right decisions and choosing the right path for your life. God knows the difficulties and challenges of this life, and that's why He sent Jesus.

2. It is okay to ask for help. Your Father in Heaven is waiting to assist you in every area of your life, and all you have to do is ASK.

3. List some ways below that you can use some assistance from the Throne. As long as your requests <u>line up</u> with His plan and purpose for your life, you can believe without a shadow of a doubt and receive your answers.

_____
_____
_____
_____
_____
_____
_____
_____
_____
_____
_____
_____
_____
_____
_____
_____
_____

Notes

Notes

Day Twenty-Nine

Today's Reading: Proverbs Chapter 29

A man who remains stiff-necked after many rebukes will suddenly be destroyed —without remedy. **2** When the righteous thrive, the people rejoice; when the wicked rule, the people groan. **3** A man who loves wisdom brings joy to his father, but a companion of prostitutes squanders his wealth. **4** By justice a king gives a country stability, but one who is greedy for bribes tears it down. **5** Whoever flatters his neighbor is spreading a net for his feet. **6** An evil man is snared by his own sin, but a righteous one can sing and be glad. **7** The righteous care about justice for the poor, but the wicked have no such concern. **8** Mockers stir up a city, but wise men turn away anger. **9** If a wise man goes to court with a fool, the fool rages and scoffs, and there is no peace. **10** Bloodthirsty men hate a man of integrity and seek to kill the upright. **11** A fool gives full vent to his anger, but a wise man keeps himself under control. **12** If a ruler listens to lies, all his officials become wicked. **13** The poor man and the oppressor have this in common: The Lord gives sight to the eyes of both. **14** If a king judges the poor with fairness, his throne will always be secure. **15** The rod of correction imparts wisdom, but a child left to himself disgraces his mother. **16** When the wicked thrive, so does sin, but the righteous will see their downfall. **17** Discipline your son, and he will give you peace; he will bring delight to your soul. **18** Where there is no revelation, the people cast off restraint; but blessed is he who keeps the law. **19** A servant cannot be corrected by mere words; though he understands, he will not respond. **20** Do you see a man who speaks in haste? There is more hope for a fool than for him. **21** If a man pampers his servant from youth, he will bring grief in the end. **22** An angry man stirs up dissension, and a hot-tempered one commits many sins. **23** A man's pride brings him low, but a man of lowly spirit gains honor. **24** The accomplice of a thief is his own enemy; he is put under oath and dare not testify. **25** Fear of man will prove to be a snare, but whoever trusts in the Lord is kept safe. **26** Many seek an audience with a ruler, but it is from the Lord that man gets justice. **27** The righteous detest the dishonest; the wicked detest the upright.

Today's Scripture: "A man's pride brings him low, but a man of lowly spirit gains honor." (Proverbs 29:23)

Today's Wisdom: Pride goes before destruction, a haughty spirit before a fall. (Proverbs 16:18)

Today's Spiritual Mindset: A prideful heart brings humiliation, but a man who is humble in spirit will gain honor from God and man.

Spiritual Mindset Journal: As Believers, you have to be humble in spirit. You have to be role models in the Kingdom of God. Pride and arrogance are not godly characteristics, but are true signs that destruction is soon to follow. Father, let me be a true representative to Your Kingdom. Let me be more like YOU and less like me.

Think of a time in your life when you were driven solely by pride or arrogance. What was the outcome?

Spiritual Mindset Action Plan: There is a big difference between the pride that God hates and the pride we feel when we have done our best at something, whether at work, at school, or in church. God hates the pride that stems from self-righteousness because it is a hindrance to seeking Him.

Pride has kept sinners from receiving Jesus as their Lord and Savior, as well as admitting their sinful ways and the fact that they are nothing without God. Pride is sinful because we give glory to ourselves, when in essence it is God who deserves ALL of the glory. Pride is self-worship.

We must acknowledge daily that all our accomplishments in the world would not have been possible if it were not for God enabling and sustaining us.

Day Twenty-Nine Worksheet

"For who sees anything different in you? What do you have that you did not receive? If then you received it, why do you boast as if you did not receive it?" (1 Corinthians 4:7)

1. What are the things in your life that you boast about instead of giving God the glory because He alone deserves it? List them below.

2. God does not like us taking the credit for the things that He has done in our lives. Now is a good time to repent and give Him the glory for ALL the things that He has done, the things that He is doing, and the things that He is going to do in your life.

Notes

Notes

Notes

DAY THIRTY

Today's Reading: Proverbs Chapter 30

The sayings of Agur son of Jakeh – an oracle: This man declared to Ithiel, to Ithiel and to Ucal: **2** "I am the most ignorant of men; I do not have a man's understanding. **3** I have not learned wisdom, nor have I knowledge of the Holy One.   **4** Who has gone up to heaven and come down? Who has gathered up the wind in the hollow of his hands? Who has wrapped up the waters in his cloak? Who has established all the ends of the earth? What is his name, and the name of his son? Tell me if you know! **5** "Every word of God is flawless; he is a shield to those who take refuge in him. **6** Do not add to his words, or he will rebuke you and prove you a liar. **7** "Two things I ask of you, O Lord; do not refuse me before I die: **8** Keep falsehood and lies far from me; give me neither poverty nor riches, but give me only my daily bread. **9** Otherwise, I may have too much and disown you and say, 'Who is the Lord?' Or I may become poor and steal, and so dishonor the name of my God. **10** "Do not slander a servant to his master, or he will curse you, and you will pay for it. **11** "There are those who curse their fathers and do not bless their mothers; **12** those who are pure in their own eyes and yet are not cleansed of their filth; **13** those whose eyes are ever so haughty, whose glances are so disdainful; **14** those whose teeth are swords and whose jaws are set with knives to devour the poor from the earth, the needy from among mankind. **15** "The leech has two daughters, 'Give! Give!' They cry. "There are three things that are never satisfied, four that never say 'Enough!': **16** the grave, the barren womb, land, which is never satisfied with water, and fire, which never says, 'Enough!' **17** "The eye that mocks a father, that scorns obedience to a mother, will be pecked out by the ravens of the valley, will be eaten by the vultures. **18** "There are three things that are too amazing for me, four that I do not understand: **19** the way of an eagle in the sky, the way of a snake on a rock, the way of a ship on the high seas, and the way of a man with a maiden. **20** "This is the way of an adulteress: She eats and wipes her mouth and says, 'I've done nothing wrong.' **21** "Under three things the earth trembles, under four it cannot bear up: **22** a servant who becomes king, a fool who is full of food, **23** an unloved woman who is married, and a maidservant who displaces her mistress. **24** "Four things on earth are small, yet they are extremely wise: **25** Ants are creatures of little strength, yet they store up their food in the summer; **26** coneys are creatures of little power, yet they make their home in the crags; **27** locusts have no king, yet they advance together in ranks; **28** a lizard can be caught with the hand, yet it is found in kings' palaces. **29** "There are three things that are stately in their stride, four that move with stately bearing: **30** a lion, mighty among beasts, who retreats before nothing; **31** a strutting rooster, a he-goat, and a king with his army around him. **32** "If you have played the fool and exalted yourself, or if you have planned evil, clap your hand over your mouth! **33** For as churning the milk produces butter, and as twisting the nose produces blood, so stirring up anger produces strife."

Today's Scripture: "Do not slander a servant to his master, or he will curse you, and you will pay for it." (Proverbs 30:10)

Today's Wisdom: Do not meddle in other people's business if you do not want people meddling in yours.

Today's Spiritual Mindset: There is no godly cause for accusing or slandering another person. If you do, you will bring judgment upon yourself.

Spiritual Mindset Journal: We must live peaceably in our own families and not give disturbance to others through gossip, scandal, and backbiting. We must always behave with quietness in our neighborhoods, towns, and cities as we pursue peace, honesty, and godliness in our lives.

Are there any opportunities in your home, church, or business where you can be the agent of change? Even though it is not popular to do so, do you see an opportunity to embark on change not in your own strength, but in God's strength?

_____
_____
_____
_____
_____
_____
_____
_____
_____
_____
_____
_____
_____
_____
_____
_____
_____
_____
_____
_____
_____
_____
_____
_____
_____

Spiritual Mindset Action Plan: Today, I will focus on minding my own business and not interfere and judge other people on theirs. A man or woman should continually employ himself in four areas with all his might. They are the law, good works, prayer, and the business of life.

Day Thirty Worksheet

Write a short sentence below that will help to remind you to pursue peace, honesty, and godliness that will contribute to making you a better person, employee, entrepreneur, and believer at home, work, business, or church.

Notes

Notes

Notes

DAY THIRTY-ONE

Today's Reading: Proverbs Chapter 31

The saying of King Lemuel —an oracle his mother taught him: **2** "O my son, O son of my womb, O son of my vows, **3** do not spend your strength on women, your vigor on those who ruin kings. **4** "It is not for kings, O Lemuel — not for kings to drink wine, not for rulers to crave beer, **5** lest they drink and forget what the law decrees, and deprive all the oppressed of their rights. **6** Give beer to those who are perishing, wine to those who are in anguish; **7** let them drink and forget their poverty and remember their misery no more. **8** "Speak up for those who cannot speak for themselves, for the rights of all who are destitute. **9** Speak up and judge fairly; defend the rights of the poor and needy." **10** A wife of noble character who can find? She is worth far more than rubies. **11** Her husband has full confidence in her and lacks nothing of value. **12** She brings him good, not harm, all the days of her life. **13** She selects wool and flax and works with eager hands. **14** She is like the merchant ships, bringing her food from afar. **15** She gets up while it is still dark; she provides food for her family and portions for her servant girls. **16** She considers a field and buys it; out of her earnings she plants a vineyard. **17** She sets about her work vigorously; her arms are strong for her tasks. **18** She sees that her trading is profitable, and her lamp does not go out at night. **19** In her hand she holds the distaff and grasps the spindle with her fingers. **20** She opens her arms to the poor and extends her hands to the needy. **21** When it snows, she has no fear for her household; for all of them are clothed in scarlet. **22** She makes coverings for her bed; she is clothed in fine linen and purple. **23** Her husband is respected at the city gate, where he takes his seat among the elders of the land. **24** She makes linen garments and sells them, and supplies the merchants with sashes. **25** She is clothed with strength and dignity; she can laugh at the days to come. **26** She speaks with wisdom, and faithful instruction is on her tongue. **27** She watches over the affairs of her household and does not eat the bread of idleness. **28** Her children arise and call her blessed; her husband also, and he praises her: **29** "Many women do noble things, but you surpass them all." **30** Charm is deceptive, and beauty is fleeting; but a woman who fears the Lord is to be praised. **31** Give her the reward she has earned, and let her works bring her praise at the city gate.

Today Scripture Reading: "Charm is deceptive and beauty is fleeting; but a woman who fears the Lord is to be praised." (Proverbs 31:30)

Today's Wisdom: The husband of a virtuous woman is well-respected among the leaders. Her influence is evident in her home and extends to all who are associated with her.

Today's Spiritual Mindset: Virtue has many more admirers than it has followers. Do you follow or admire individuals who exhibit virtue or excellence?

Spiritual Mindset Journal: The characteristics of virtuous women state that they have a responsibility to be financially savvy and business literate. They are physical but not masculine. They have high standards but are not perfect. They run their home but are not consumed by the tedious chores that can stifle their creative imagination. They are God-fearing and people-loving. They cover their husbands and children both in the literal and spiritual sense. When you mess with a Proverbs 31 woman, you'd better ask God to have mercy on your soul.

Write the names of at least ten (10) virtuous women in your life. If you cannot think of any, maybe it's time to share this *31-Day Spiritual Mindset Makeover Journal* with them and see how God will transform their lives as they journey through the Book of Proverbs.

_____
_____
_____
_____
_____
_____
_____
_____
_____
_____
_____
_____
_____
_____
_____
_____
_____
_____
_____
_____
_____
_____
_____
_____
_____

Spiritual Mindset Action Plan: Father, help me to model my life as that of a "virtuous" man/woman. I submit myself to Your will. Mold me and develop me into the woman/man of God that You have called me to be. Let me be a Blessing in my home, community, country, and the world over. Amen!

Day Thirty-One Worksheet

The Book of Proverbs has given you God's Wisdom for every area of your life. Now you know that God's ultimate desire is that you live your life and live it more abundantly.

Based on what you have learned, please take some time to answer the following questions below and watch your life transform as you continue to read and document your journey through the Book of Proverbs.

1. Define your understanding of success based on what you have learned from the scriptures.

   _____
   _____
   _____
   _____
   _____

2. What are your treasures in heaven? What are your treasures on earth? What does the Bible have to say about these?

   _____
   _____
   _____
   _____
   _____

3. Name five things that Proverbs tells you to do to be successful.

   _____
   _____

4. What are your life goals? How will you determine your success?

5. How does your goal stand up to the biblical principles that you have learned?

6. List all the steps that you are taking now to pursue success.

Notes

Notes

Notes

Graduation Day

"He who began a good work in you will carry it on to completion until the day of Christ Jesus." (Philippians 1:6)

Congratulations on completing the *31-Day Spiritual Mindset Makeover Journal...A Journey Through the Book of Proverbs.* As you can see, the Spiritual Mindset Makeover is a lifelong journey to spiritual health. Our vision is that this journey will help you jump-start a process of transformation that will bless your life abundantly as well as the lives of those around you. We hope and pray that your experience with this book will produce spiritual growth and wisdom beyond your years.

The Word of God promises that you progress from glory to glory: *"And we, who with unveiled faces all reflect the Lord's glory, are being transformed into his likeness with ever-increasing glory, which comes from the Lord, who is the Spirit."* (2 Corinthians 3:18).

God Bless you as you begin a new month and a new journey through the Book of Proverbs!

Affirmations and Visualizations

Affirmations and visualizations are a very important part of our daily lives. They help us identify the things that we want in our lives, so that we give little attention and focus to the things that we do not want. Unfortunately, most people do not know what they want, and that is why they continue to go through life without the focus and guidance that are necessary to arrive at their destination to greatness.

Not knowing what you want from this life or how to get to where you want to be makes it virtually impossible to arrive. However, I believe that even if you do not know what you want or how to get there, you can put God in charge and He will take you from where you are to where He created you to be, one day at a time.

I promise that He will be very patient with you. He will discipline you and challenge you along the way. If you believe in your heart that you deserve ALL the Blessings and joys that life has to offer, then you are ready for the next level in your life. Every day is full of possibilities and challenges, but you can harness the possibility and overcome every challenge if you stay focused on His Word.

Below are just a few of God's promises for your life if you entrust it to Him completely. Start every day empowered by repeating the Affirmations of "The Power of...I AM" to keep you focused on God and His promises for your life. Remember, your importance will not stem from what you have made of yourself, but of what Christ has made of you. Below are 26 sentences that I want you to repeat as many times as it takes to convince yourself that you are who He says you are: "Because I am a child of the Most High God, I AM _____."
Now it is your job to live out your identity today as a child of the King!

THE POWER OF....I AM

I AM	...Anointed (Exodus 40:15)
I AM	...Blessed (Genesis 12:3)
I AM	...Chosen (John 15:16)
I AM	...Delivered (Exodus 14:13)
I AM	...Exceedingly Prosperous (Genesis 30:43)
I AM	...Fearless (Psalms 27:1)
I AM	...Guided (Psalm 32:8)
I AM	...Healed (Isaiah 53:5)
I AM	...Image of God (Genesis 1:27)
I AM	...Justified (Romans 8:30)
I AM	...Kingdom Builder (Exodus 19:6)
I AM	...Light of the World (Matthew 5:14)
I AM	...Morning Star (Revelation 22:16)
I AM	...New Creation (2 Corinthians 5;17)
I AM	...Overcomer (Jeremiah 1:19)
I AM	...Protected (Psalm 34:7)
I AM	...Qualified (Colossians 1:12)
I AM	...Redeemed (Psalm 107:2)
I AM	...Saved (Acts 16:31)
I AM	...Transformed (Romans 12:12)
I AM	...Under Grace (Romans 6:14)
I AM	...Victorious (1 Corinthians 15:57)
I AM	...Waiting on the Lord (Psalm 27:14)
I AM	..eXample (John 13:15)
I AM	...Your Workmanship (Ephesians 2:10)
I AM	...Zealous for God (1King 19:10)

One-Year Bible Reading Plan

Below is an outline to help you read the Bible in one year. This monthly reading plan is designed to help you delve into the Bible daily as you journey through God's Word. On the seventh day, you can take a day off or use the time to catch up to any missed days so you do not fall behind.

You can begin at any time during the year and this plan is designed to keep you reading the Bible year after year. Before you begin any scripture reading, be sure to ask God to minister to you and give you revelation as you spend your time in His Word.

31 Day Spiritual Mindset Makeover Bible Reading Plan - January

	1	2	3	4	5
	January 1 - Day 1 Genesis Chapters 1 and 2	January 2 - Day 2 Genesis Chapters 3, 4, and 5	January 3 - Day 3 Genesis Chapters 6, 7, 8, and 9	January 4 - Day 4 Genesis Chapters 10 and 11	January 5 - Day 5 Genesis Chapters 12, 13, and 14

6	7	8	9	10	11	12
January 6 - Day 6 Genesis Chapters 15, 16, and 17	January 7 - Day 7 Time of Reflection. Get caught up on any missed bible reading this week.	January 8 - Day 8 Genesis Chapters 18, 19, and 20	January 9 - Day 9 Genesis Chapters 21, 22, 23, and 24	January 10 - Day 10 Genesis Chapters 25 and 26	January 11 - Day 11 Genesis Chapters 27, 28, 29, 30, and 31	January 12 - Day 12 Genesis Chapters 32, 33, 34, 35, and 36

13	14	15	16	17	18	19
January 13 - Day 13 Genesis Chapters 37, 38, 39, and 40	January 14 - Day 14 Time of Reflection. Get caught up on any missed bible reading this week.	January 15 - Day 15 Genesis Chapters 41, 42, 43, and 44	January 16 - Day 16 Genesis Chapters 45, 46, and 47	January 17 - Day 17 Genesis 48, 49, and 50	January 18 - Day 18 Exodus Chapters 1 and 2	January 19 - Day 19 Exodus Chapters 3, 4, 5, and 6

20	21	22	23	24	25	26
January 20 - Day 20 Exodus Chapters 7, 8, 9, and 10	January 21 - Day 21 Time of Reflection. Get caught up on any missed bible reading this week.	January 22 - Day 22 Exodus Chapters 11 and 12	January 23 - Day 23 Exodus Chapters 13, 14, and 15	January 24 - Day 24 Exodus Chapters 16, 17, and 18	January 25 - Day 25 Exodus Chapters 19 and 20	January 26 - Day 26 Exodus Chapters 21, 22, 23, and 24

27	28	29	30	31
January 27 - Day 27 Exodus 25, 26, and 27	January 28 - Day 28 Time of Reflection. Get caught up on any missed bible reading this week.	January 29 - Day 29 Exodus Chapters 28, 29, 30, and 31	January 30 - Day 30 Exodus Chapters 32, 33, and 34	January 31 - Day 31 Exodus Chapters 35, 36, 37, 38, 39, and 40

Notes:

Please continue to read the Spiritual Mindset Makeover Journal and document your daily experiences. For continued spiritual growth, please include the daily bible reading plan as part of your daily devotional time.

31 Day Spiritual Mindset Makeover Bible Reading Plan - February

Sun	Mon	Tue	Wed	Thu	Fri	Sat
					February 1 - Day 32 Leviticus Chapters 1, 2, and 3	February 2 - Day 33 Leviticus Chapters 4, 5, 6, and 7
February 3 - Day 34 Leviticus Chapters 8, 9, and 10	February 4 - Day 35 Leviticus Chapters 11, 12, 13, 14, and 15	February 5 - Day 36 Leviticus Chapters 16 and 17	February 6 - Day 37 Leviticus Chapters 18, 19, and 20	February 7 - Day 38 Time of Reflection. Get caught up on any missed bible reading this week.	February 8 - Day 39 Leviticus Chapters 21, 22, and 23	February 9 - Day 40 Leviticus Chapters 24, 25, 26, and 27
February 10 - Day 41 Numbers Chapters 1, 2, 3, and 4	February 11 - Day 42 Numbers Chapters 5, 6, 7, and 8	February 12 - Day 43 Numbers Chapters 9, 10, 11, and 12	February 13 - Day 44 Numbers 13, 14, 15, and 16	February 14 - Day 45 Time of Reflection. Get caught up on any missed bible reading this week.	February 15 - Day 46 Numbers 17, 18, 19, and 20	February 16 - Day 47 Numbers Chapters 21, 22, 23, 24, and 25
February 17 - Day 48 Numbers Chapters 26, 27, 28, 29, and 30	February 18 - Day 49 Numbers 31, 32, and 33	February 19 - Day 50 Numbers 34, 35, and 36	February 20 - Day 51 Deuteronomy Chapters 1, 2, 3, and 4	February 21 - Day 52 Time of Reflection. Get caught up on any missed bible reading this week.	February 22 - Day 53 Deuteronomy Chapters 5, 6, and 7	February 23 - Day 54 Deuteronomy Chapters 8, 9, 10, and 11
February 24 - Day 55 Deuteronomy Chapters 12, 13, 14, 15, and 16	February 25 - Day 56 Deuteronomy Chapters 17, 18, 19, and 20	February 26 - Day 57 Deuteronomy Chapters 21, 22, 23, 24, 25, and 26	February 27 - Day 58 Deuteronomy Chapters 27, 28, 29, 30, 31, 32, 33, and 34	February 28 - Day 59 Time of Reflection. Get caught up on any missed bible reading this week.		

Notes:

Please continue to read the Spiritual Mindset Makeover Journal and document your daily experiences. For continued spiritual growth, please include the daily bible reading plan as part of your daily devotional time.

31 Day Spiritual Mindset Makeover Bible Reading Plan - March

SUNDAY	MONDAY	TUESDAY	WEDNESDAY	THURSDAY	FRIDAY	SATURDAY
					March 1 - Day 60 Joshua Chapters 1, 2, 3, 4, and 5	March 2 - Day 61 Joshua Chapters 6, 7, and 8
March 3 - Day 62 Joshua Chapters 9, 10, 11, and 12	March 4 - Day 63 Joshua Chapters 13, 14, 15, 16, and 17	March 5 - Day 64 Joshua Chapters 18, 19, 20, and 21	March 6 - Day 65 Joshua Chapters 22, 23, and 24	March 7 - Day 66 Time of Reflection. Get caught up on any missed bible reading this week.	March 8 - Day 67 Judges Chapters 1, 2, 3, 4 and 5	March 9 - Day 68 Judges Chapters 6, 7, and 8
March 10 - Day 69 Judges Chapters 9, 10, 11, and 12	March 11 - Day 70 Judges Chapters 13, 14, 15, and 16	March 12 - Day 71 Judges Chapters 17, 18, 19, 20, and 21	March 13 - Day 72 Ruth Chapters 1, 2, 3, and 4	March 14 - Day 73 Time of Reflection. Get caught up on any missed bible reading this week.	March 15 - Day 74 1 Samuel Chapters 1, 2, and 3	March 16 - Day 75 1 Samuel Chapters 4, 5, 6, 7, and 8
March 17 - Day 76 1 Samuel Chapters 9, 10, 11, and 12	March 18 - Day 77 1 Samuel Chapters 13, 14, and 15	March 19 - Day 78 1 Samuel Chapters 16, 17, 18, and 19	March 20 - Day 79 1 Samuel Chapters 20, 21, 22, and 23	March 21 - Day 80 Time of Reflection. Get caught up on any missed bible reading this week.	March 22 - Day 81 1 Samuel Chapters 24, 25, and 26	March 23 - Day 82 1 Samuel Chapters 27, 28, 29, 30, and 31
March 24 - Day 83 2 Samuel Chapters 1, 2, 3, and 4	March 25 - Day 84 2 Samuel Chapters 5, 6, and 7	March 26 - Day 85 2 Samuel Chapters 8, 9, and 10	March 27 - Day 86 2 Samuel Chapters 11, 12, 13, and 14	March 28 - Day 87 Time of Reflection. Get caught up on any missed bible reading this week.	March 29 - Day 88 2 Samuel Chapters 15, 16, 17, and 18	March 30 - Day 89 2 Samuel Chapters 19 and 20
March 31 - Day 90 2 Samuel Chapters 21, 22, 23, and 24		Notes:				

Please continue to read the Spiritual Mindset Makeover Journal and document your daily experiences. For continued spiritual growth, please include the daily bible reading plan as part of your daily devotional time.

31 Day Spiritual Mindset Makeover Bible Reading Plan - April

	1	2	3	4	5	6
	April 1 - Day 91 1 Kings Chapters 1, 2, 3, and 4	April 2 - Day 92 1 Kings Chapters 5, 6, 7, and 8	April 3 - Day 93 1 Kings Chapters 9, 10, and 11	April 4 - Day 94 1 Kings Chapters 12, 13, 14, 15, and 16	April 5 - Day 95 1 Kings Chapters 17, 18, and 19	April 6 - Day 96 1 Kings Chapters 20, 21, and 22
7	8	9	10	11	12	13
April 7 - Day 97 Time of Reflection. Get caught up on any missed bible reading this week.	April 8 - Day 98 2 Kings Chapters 1, 2, and 3	April 9 - Day 99 2 Kings Chapters 4, 5, 6, 7, and 8	April 10 - Day 100 2 Kings Chapters 9, 10, 11, and 12	April 11 - Day 101 2 Kings Chapters 13, 14, 15, 16, and 17	April 12 - Day 102 2 Kings Chapters 18, 19, 20, and 21	April 13 - Day 103 2 Kings Chapters 22, 23, 24, and 25
14	15	16	17	18	19	20
April 14 - Day 104 Time of Reflection. Get caught up on any missed bible reading this week.	April 15 - Day 105 1 Chronicles Chapters 1, 2, 3, 4, 5, 6, 7, 8, and 9	April 16 - Day 106 1 Chronicles Chapters 10, 11, 12, 13, 14, 15, and 16	April 17 - Day 107 1 Chronicles Chapters 17, 18, 19, 20, and 21	April 18 - Day 108 1 Chronicles Chapters 22, 23, 24, 25, 26, and 27	April 19 - Day 109 1 Chronicles Chapters 28 and 29	April 20 - Day 110 2 Chronicles Chapters 1, 2, 3, 4, and 5
21	22	23	24	25	26	27
April 21 - Day 111 Time of Reflection. Get caught up on any missed bible reading this week.	April 22 - Day 112 2 Chronicles Chapters 6, 7, 8, and 9	April 23 - Day 113 2 Chronicles Chapters 10, 11, and 12	April 24 - Day 114 2 Chronicles Chapters 13, 14, 15, and 16	April 25 - Day 115 2 Chronicles Chapters 17, 18, 19, and 20	April 26 - Day 116 2 Chronicles Chapters 21, 22, 23, 24, and 25	April 27 - Day 117 2 Chronicles Chapters 26, 27, and 28
28	29	30				
April 28 - Day 118 Time of Reflection. Get caught up on any missed bible reading this week.	April 29 - Day 119 2 Chronicles Chapters 29, 30, 31, and 32	April 30 - Day 120 2 Chronicles Chapters 33, 34, 35, and 36				

Notes

Please continue to read the Spiritual Mindset Makeover Journal and document your daily experiences. For continued spiritual growth, please include the daily bible reading plan as part of your daily devotional time.

31 Day Spiritual Mindset Makeover Bible Reading Plan - May

		1	2	3	4
		May 1 - Day 121 Ezra Chapters 1, 2, and 3	May 2 - Day 122 Ezra Chapters 4, 5, and 6	May 3 - Day 123 Ezra Chapters 7 and 8	May 4 - Day 124 Ezra Chapters 9 and 10
5	6	7	8	9	10	11
May 5 - 125 Nehemiah Chapters 1 and 2	May 6 - Day 126 Nehemiah Chapters 3 and 4	May 7 - Day 127 Time of Reflection. Get caught up on any missed bible reading this week.	May 8 - Day 128 Nehemiah Chapters 5, 6, and 7	May 9 - Day 129 Nehemiah Chapters 8, 9, and 10	May 10 - Day 130 Nehemiah Chapters 11, 12, and 13	May 11 - Day 131 Ester Chapters 1 and 2
12	13	14	15	16	17	18
May 12 - Day 132 Ester Chapters 3 and 4	May 13 - Day 133 Ester Chapters 5, 6, and 7	May 14 - Day 134 Time of Reflection. Get caught up on any missed bible reading this week.	May 15 - Day 135 Ester Chapters 8, 9, and 10	May 16 - Day 136 Job Chapters 1, 2, and 3	May 17 - Day 137 Job Chapters 4, 5, 6, and 7	May 18 - Day 138 Job Chapters 8, 9, and 10
19	20	21	22	23	24	25
May 19 - Day 139 Job Chapters 11, 12, 13, and 14	May 20 - Day 140 Job Chapters 15, 16, and 17	May 21 - Day 141 Time of Reflection. Get caught up on any missed bible reading this week.	May 22 - Day 142 Job Chapters 18 and 19	May 23 - Day 143 Job Chapters 20 and 21	May 24 - Day 144 Job Chapters 22, 23, and 24	May 25 - Day 145 Job Chapters 25, 26, 27, and 28
26	27	28	29	30	31	
May 26 - Day 146 Job Chapters 29, 30, and 31	May 27 - Day 147 Job Chapters 32, 33, and 34	May 28 - Day 148 Time of Reflection. Get caught up on any missed bible reading this week.	May 29 - Day 149 Job Chapters 35, 36, and 37	May 30 - Day 150 Job Chapters 38 and 39	May 31 - Day 151 Job Chapters 40, 41, and 42	

Notes:

Please continue to read the Spiritual Mindset Makeover Journal and document your daily experiences. For continued spiritual growth, please include the daily bible reading plan as part of your daily devotional time.

31 Day Spiritual Mindset Makeover Bible Reading Plan - June

						1 June 1 - Day 152 Psalms Chapters 1, 2, 3, 4, 5, and 6
2 June 2 - Day 153 Psalms Chapters 7, 8, 9, 10, 11, and 12	3 June 3 - Day 154 Psalms Chapters 13, 14, 15, 16, 17, and 18	4 June 4 - Day 155 Psalms Chapters 19, 20, 21, 22, 23, and 24	5 June 5 - Day 156 Psalms Chapters 25, 26, 27, 28, 29, and 30	6 June 6 - Day 157 Psalms Chapters 31, 32, 33, 34, and 35	7 June 7 - Day 158 Time of Reflection. Get caught up on any missed bible reading this week.	8 June 8 - Day 159 Psalms Chapters 36, 37, 38, 39, 40, and 41
9 June 9 - Day 160 Psalms Chapters 42, 43, 44, 45, 46, 47, 48, and 49	10 June 10 - Day 161 Psalms Chapters 50, 51, 52, 53, and 54	11 June 11 - Day 162 Psalms Chapters 55, 56, 57, 58, and 59	12 June 12 - Day 163 Psalms Chapters 60, 61, 62, 63, 64, 65, and 66	13 June 13 - Day 164 Psalms Chapters 67, 68, 69, 70, 71, and 72	14 June 14 - Day 165 Time of Reflection. Get caught up on any missed bible reading this week.	15 June 15 - Day 166 Psalms Chapters 73, 74, 75, 76, and 77
16 June 16 - Day 167 Psalms Chapters 78, 79, 80, 81, 82, and 83	17 June 17 - Day 168 Psalms Chapters 84, 85, 86, 87, 88, and 89	18 June 18 - Day 169 Psalms Chapters 90, 91, 92, 93, 94, 95, 96, and 97	19 June 19 - Day 170 Psalms Chapters 98, 99, 100, 101, 102, and 103	20 June 20 - Day 171 Psalms Chapters 104, 105 and 106	21 June 21 - Day 172 Time of Reflection. Get caught up on any missed bible reading this week.	22 June 22 - Day 173 Psalms Chapters 107, 108, 109, and 110
23 June 23 - Day 174 Psalms Chapters 111, 112, 113, 114, 115, 116, 117, and 118	24 June 24 - Day 175 Psalms Chapter 119	25 June 25 - Day 176 Psalms Chapters 120, 121, 122, 123, 124, 125, 126, and 127	26 June 26 - Day 177 Psalms Chapters 128, 129, 130, 131, 132, 133, and 134	27 June 27 - Day 178 Psalms Chapters 135, 136, 137, 138, and 139	28 June 28 - Day 179 Time of Reflection. Get caught up on any missed bible reading this week.	29 June 29 - Day 180 Psalms Chapters 140, 141, 142, 143, 144, and 145
30 June 30 - Day 181 Psalms Chapters 146, 147, 148, 149, and 150	Notes:					

Please continue to read the Spiritual Mindset Makeover Journal and document your daily experiences. For continued spiritual growth, please include the daily bible reading plan as part of your daily devotional time.

31 Day Spiritual Mindset Makeover Bible Reading Plan - July

	1	2	3	4	5	6
	July 1 - Day 182 Proverbs Chapters 1, 2, 3, and 4	July 2 - Day 183 Proverbs Chapters 5, 6, 7, 8, and 9	July 3 - Day 184 Proverbs Chapters 10, 11, 12, and 13	July 4 - Day 185 Proverbs Chapters 14, 15, 16, and 17	July 5 - Day 186 Proverbs Chapters 18, 19, 20, and 21	July 6 - Day 187 Proverbs Chapters 22, 23, and 24
7	8	9	10	11	12	13
July 7 - Day 188 Time of Reflection. Get caught up on any missed bible reading this week.	July 8 - Day 189 Proverbs Chapters 25, 26, 27, 28, and 29	July 9 - Day 190 Proverbs Chapters 30 and 31	July 10 - Day 191 Ecclesiastes Chapters 1, 2, 3, 4, 5, and 6	July 11 - Day 192 Ecclesiastes Chapters 7, 8, 9, 10, 11, and 12	July 12 - Day 193 Song of Songs Chapters 1, 2, 3, 4, 5, 6, 7, and 8	July 13 - Day 194 Isaiah Chapters 1, 2, 3, and 4
14	15	16	17	18	19	20
July 14 - Day 195 Time of Reflection. Get caught up on any missed bible reading this week.	July 15 - Day 196 Isaiah Chapters 5, 6, 7, and 8	July 16 - Day 197 Isaiah Chapters 9, 10, 11, and 12	July 17 - Day 198 Isaiah Chapters 13, 14, 15, and 16	July 18 - Day 199 Isaiah Chapters 17, 18, 19, and 20	July 19 - Day 200 Isaiah Chapters 21, 22, and 23	July 20 - Day 201 Isaiah Chapters 24, 25, 26, and 27
21	22	23	24	25	26	27
July 21 - Day 202 Time of Reflection. Get caught up on any missed bible reading this week.	July 22 - Day 203 Isaiah Chapters 28, 29, and 30	July 23 - Day 204 Isaiah Chapters 31, 32, 33, 34, and 35	July 24 - Day 205 Isaiah Chapters 36, 37, 38, and 39	July 25 - Day 206 Isaiah Chapters 40, 41, 42, and 43	July 26 - Day 207 Isaiah Chapters 44, 45, 46, 47, and 48	July 27 - Day 208 Isaiah Chapters 49, 50, and 51
28	29	30	31			
July 28 - Day 219 Time of Reflection. Get caught up on any missed bible reading this week.	July 29 - Day 210 Isaiah Chapters 52, 53, 54, 55, 56, and 57	July 30 - Day 211 Isaiah Chapters 58, 59, 60, 61, and 62	July 31 - Day 212 Isaiah Chapters 63, 64, 65, and 66			

Notes:

Please continue to read the Spiritual Mindset Makeover Journal and document your daily experiences. For continued spiritual growth, please include the daily bible reading plan as part of your daily devotional time.

31 Day Spiritual Mindset Makeover Bible Reading Plan - August

			1	2	3
			August 1 - Day 213 Jeremiah Chapters 1, 2, 3, 4, 5, and 6	August 2 - Day 214 Jeremiah Chapters 7, 8, 9, and 10	August 3 - Day 215 Jeremiah Chapters 11, 12, 13, 14, and 15
4	5	6	7	8	9	10
August 4 - Day 216 Jeremiah Chapters 16, 17, 18, 19, and 20	August 5 - Day 217 Jeremiah Chapters 21, 22, 23, 24, and 25	August 6 - Day 218 Jeremiah Chapters 26, 27, 28, and 29	August 7 - Day 219 Time of Reflection. Get caught up on any missed bible reading this week.	August 8 - Day 220 Jeremiah Chapters 30, 31, 32, and 33	August 9 - Day 221 Jeremiah Chapters 34, 35, and 36	August 10 - Day 222 Jeremiah Chapters 37, 38, and 39
11	12	13	14	15	16	17
August 11 - Day 223 Jeremiah Chapters 40, 41, 42, 43, 44, and 45	August 12 - Day 224 Jeremiah Chapters 46, 47, 48, 49, 50, 51, and 52	August 13 - Day 225 Lamentations Chapters 1, 2, 3, 4, and 5	August 14 - Day 226 Time of Reflection. Get caught up on any missed bible reading this week.	August 15 - Day 227 Ezekiel Chapters 1, 2, 3, 4, 5, and 6	August 16 - Day 228 Ezekiel Chapters 7, 8, 9, 10, and 11	August 17 - Day 229 Ezekiel Chapters 12, 13, 14, and 15
18	19	20	21	22	23	24
August 18 - Day 230 Ezekiel Chapters 16, 17, 18, and 19	August 19 - Day 231 Ezekiel Chapters 20, 21, 22, and 23	August 20 - Day 232 Ezekiel Chapters 24, 25, 26, 27, and 28	August 21 - Day 233 Time of Reflection. Get caught up on any missed bible reading this week.	August 22- Day 234 Ezekiel Chapters 29, 30, 31, and 32	August 23 - Day 235 Ezekiel Chapters 33, 34, 35, and 36	August 24 - Day 236 Ezekiel Chapters 37, 38, and 39
25	26	27	28	29	30	31
August 25 - Day 237 Ezekiel Chapters 40, 41, 42, and 43	August 26 - Day 238 Ezekiel Chapters 44, 45, 46, 47, and 48	August 27 - Day 239 Daniel Chapters 1, 2, and 3	August 28 - Day 240 Time of Reflection. Get caught up on any missed bible reading this week.	August 29 - Day 241 Daniel Chapters 4, 5, and 6	August 30 - Day 242 Daniel Chapters 7, 8, and 9	August 31 - Day 243 Daniel Chapters 10, 11, and 12

Notes:

Please continue to read the Spiritual Mindset Makeover Journal and document your daily experiences. For continued spiritual growth, please include the daily bible reading plan as part of your daily devotional time.

31 Day Spiritual Mindset Makeover Bible Reading Plan - September

	1	2	3	4	5	6	7
	September 1 Day 244 Hosea Chapters 1, 2, and 3	**September 2** Day 245 Hosea Chapters 4, 5, and 6	**September 3** Day 246 Hosea Chapters 7 and 8	**September 4** Day 247 Hosea Chapters 9, 10, and 11	**September 4** Day 248 Hosea Chapters 12, 13, and 14	**September 6** Day 249 Joel 1, 2, and 3	**September 7** Day 250 Time of Reflection. Get caught up on any missed bible reading this week.
	8	9	10	11	12	13	14
	September 8 Day 251 Amos 1 and 2	**September 9** Day 252 Amos 3, 4, and 5	**September 10** Day 253 Amos 6 and 7	**September 11** Day 254 Amos 8 and 9	**September 12** Day 255 Book of Obadiah	**September 13** Day 256 Jonah 1, 2, 3, and 4	**September 14** Day 257 Time of Reflection. Get caught up on any missed bible reading this week.
	15	16	17	18	19	20	21
	September 15 Day 258 Micah Chapters 1 and 2	**September 16** Day 259 Micah Chapters 3, 4, and 5	**September 17** Day 260 Micah Chapters 6 and 7	**September 18** Day 261 Nahum Chapters 1, 2, and 3	**September 19** Day 262 Habakkuk Chapters 1, 2, and 3	**September 20** Day 263 Zephaniah Chapters 1, 2, and 3	**September 21** Day 264 Time of Reflection. Get caught up on any missed bible reading this week.
	22	23	24	25	26	27	28
	September 22 Day 265 Haggai Chapters 1 and 2	**September 23** Day 266 Zechariah Chapters 1 and 2	**September 24** Day 267 Zechariah Chapters 3 and 4	**September 25** Day 268 Zechariah Chapters 5 and 6	**September 26** Day 269 Zechariah Chapters 7 and 8	**September 27** Day 270 Zechariah Chapters 9, 10, and 11	**September 28** Day 271 Time of Reflection. Get caught up on any missed bible reading this week.
	29	30					
	September 29 Day 272 Zechariah Chapters 12, 13, and 14	**September 30** Day 273 Malachi Chapters 1, 2, 3, and 4					

Notes:

Please continue to read the Spiritual Mindset Makeover Journal and document your daily experiences. For continued spiritual growth, please include the daily bible reading plan as part of your daily devotional time.

31 Day Spiritual Mindset Makeover Bible Reading Plan - October

	1	2	3	4	5
	October 1 - Day 274 Matthew Chapters 1, 2, 3, and 4	October 2 - Day 275 Matthew Chapters 5, 6, and 7	October 3 - Day 276 Matthew Chapters 8, 9, 10, and 11	October 4 - Day 277 Matthew Chapters 12, 13, 14, and 15	October 5 - Day 278 Matthew Chapters 16, 17, 18, and 19
6	7	8	9	10	11	12
October 6 - Day 279 Matthew Chapters 20, 21, 22, and 23	October 7 - Day 280 Time of Reflection. Get caught up on any missed bible reading this week.	October 8 - Day 281 Matthew Chapters 24 and 25	October 9 - Day 282 Matthew Chapters 26, 27 and 28	October 10 - Day 283 Mark Chapters 1, 2, and 3	October 11 - Day 284 Mark Chapters 4, 5, 6, and 7	October 12 - Day 285 Mark Chapters 8, 9, and 10
13	14	15	16	17	18	19
October 13 - Day 286 Mark Chapters 11, 12, and 13	October 14 - Day 287 Time of Reflection. Get caught up on any missed bible reading this week.	October 15 - Day 288 Mark Chapters 14, 15, and 16	October 16 - Day 289 Luke Chapters 1 and 2	October 17 - Day 290 Luke Chapters 3, 4, 5, and 6	October 18 - Day 291 Luke Chapters 7, 8, and 9	October 19 - Day 292 Luke Chapters 10, 11, and 12
20	21	22	23	24	25	26
October 20 - Day 293 Luke Chapters 13, 14, and 15	October 21 Day 294 Time of Reflection. Get caught up on any missed bible reading this week.	October 22 - Day 295 Luke Chapters 16, 17, and 18	October 23 - Day 296 Luke Chapters 19, 20, and 21	October 24 - Day 297 Luke Chapters 22, 23, and 24	October 25 - Day 298 John Chapters 1 and 2	October 26 - Day 299 John Chapters 3, 4, and 5
27	28	29	30	31		
October 27 - Day 300 John Chapters 6, 7, and 8	October 28 - Day 301 Time of Reflection. Get caught up on any missed bible reading this week.	October 29 - Day 302 John Chapters 9, 10, 11, and 12	October 30 - Day 303 John Chapters 13, 14, 15, 16, and 17	October 31 - Day 304 John Chapters 18, 19, 20, and 21		

Notes:

Please continue to read the Spiritual Mindset Makeover Journal and document your daily experiences. For continued spiritual growth, please include the daily bible reading plan as part of your daily devotional time.

31 Day Spiritual Mindset Makeover Bible Reading Plan - November

Sunday	Monday	Tuesday	Wednesday	Thursday	Friday	Saturday
	November 1 Day 305 Acts Chapters 1, 2, 3 and 4	November 2 Day 306 Acts Chapters 5, 6, and 7				
November 3 Day 307 Acts Chapters 8 and 9	November 4 Day 308 Acts Chapters 10, 11, and 12	November 5 Day 309 Acts Chapters 13, 14, and 15	November 6 Day 310 Acts Chapters 16, 17, and 18	November 7 Day 311 Time of Reflection. Get caught up on any missed bible reading this week.	November 8 Day 312 Acts Chapters 19 and 20	November 9 Day 313 Acts Chapters 21, 22, and 23
November 10 Day 314 Acts 24, 25, and 26	November 11 Day 315 Acts 27 and 28	November 12 Day 316 Romans 1, 2, and 3	November 13 Day 317 Romans 4 and 5	November 14 Day 318 Time of Reflection. Get caught up on any missed bible reading this week.	November 15 Day 319 Romans 6, 7 and 8	November 16 Day 320 Romans 9, 10, and 11
November 17 Day 321 Romans 12, 13, 14, 15, and 16	November 18 Day 322 1 Corinthians Chapters 1, 2, 3, 4, 5, and 6	November 19 Day 323 1 Corinthians Chapters 7, 8, 9, 10, and 11	November 20 Day 324 1 Corinthians Chapters 12, 13, and 14	November 21 Day 325 Time of Reflection. Get caught up on any missed bible reading this week.	November 22 Day 326 1 Corinthians Chapters 15 and 16	November 23 Day 327 2 Corinthians Chapters 1, 2, 3, 4 and 5
November 24 Day 328 2 Corinthians 6, 7, 8, and 9	November 25 Day 329 2 Corinthians Chapters 10, 11, 12, and 13	November 26 Day 330 Galatians Chapters 1, 2, 3, 4, 5, and 6	November 27 Day 331 Ephisians Chapters 1, 2, 3, 4, 5, and 6	November 28 Day 332 Time of Reflection. Get caught up on any missed bible reading this week.	November 29 Day 333 Philippians Chapters 1, 2, 3, and 4	November 30 Day 334 Colossians Chapters 1, 2, 3, and 4

Notes:

Please continue to read the Spiritual Mindset Makeover Journal and document your daily experiences. For continued spiritual growth, please include the daily bible reading plan as part of your daily devotional time.

31 Day Spiritual Mindset Makeover Bible Reading Plan - December

1	2	3	4	5	6	7
December 1 Day 335 1 Thessalonians Chapters 1, 2, 3, 4, and 5	December 2 Day 336 2 Thessalonians Chapters 1, 2, and 3	December 3 Day 337 1 Timothy Chapters 1, 2, and 3	December 4 Day 338 1 Timothy Chapters 4, 5, and 6	December 5 Day 339 2 Timothy Chapters 1, 2, 3, and 4	December 6 Day 340 Titus Chapters 1, 2, and 3	December 7 Day 341 Time of Reflection. Get caught up on any missed bible reading this week.
8	9	10	11	12	13	14
December 8 Day 342 Book of Philemon	December 9 Day 343 Hebrews Chapters 1 and 2	December 10 Day 344 Hebrews Chapters 3 and 4	December 11 Day 345 Hebrews Chapters 5, 6, and 7	December 12 Day 346 Hebrews Chapters 8, 9, and 10	December 13 Day 347 Hebrews 11, 12, and 13	December 14 Day 348 Time of Reflection. Get caught up on any missed bible reading this week.
15	16	17	18	19	20	21
December 15 Day 349 James Chapters 1, 2, 3, 4, and 5	December 16 Day 350 1 Peter Chapters 1, 2, 3, 4, and 5	December 17 Day 351 2 Peter Chapters 1, 2, and 3	December 18 Day 352 1 John Chapters 1, 2, 3, 4, and 5	December 19 Day 353 Book of 2 John	December 20 Day 354 Book of 3 John	December 21 Day 355 Time of Reflection. Get caught up on any missed bible reading this week.
22	23	24	25	26	27	28
December 22 Day 356 Book of Jude	December 23 Day 357 Revelation Chapters 1, 2, and 3	December 24 Day 358 Revelation Chapters 4, 5, and 6	December 25 Day 359 Matthew 1:18 - 2:12; Luke 2:1-10	December 26 Day 360 Revelation Chapters 7, 8, and 9	December 27 Day 361 Revelation Chapters 10, 11, 12, and 13	December 28 Day 362 Time of Reflection. Get caught up on any missed bible reading this week.
29	30	31				
December 29 day 363 Revelation Chapters 14, 15 and 16	December 30 Day 364 Revelation Chapters 17, 18, and 19	December 31 Day 365 Revelation Chapters 20, 21, and 22				

Notes:

Please continue to read the Spiritual Mindset Makeover Journal and document your daily experiences. For continued spiritual growth, please include the daily bible reading plan as part of your daily devotional time.

TO ORDER ADDITIONAL PRODUCTS PLEASE CONTACT:

Carlene B. Charlemagne at (973) 802-1115

PRODUCTS AND SERVICES

GOD AND BUSINESS CD/DVD

SPIRITITUAL MINDET MAKEOVER CD/DVD

31-DAY SPIRITUAL MINDSET MAKEOVER JOURNAL COMPANION CD

SPIRITUAL MINDSET MAKEOVER 2013 BIBLE READING PLAN

THE POWER OF "I AM" AFFIRMATION POSTER AND BOOKMARK

SPIRITUAL MINDSET MAKEOVER 8-WEEK COACHING PROGRAM

FOR MORE INFORMATION:
Text "IMUNLIMITED" or "IMU" to 55469

E:mail: IMUNLIMITED@ME.COM

Website: WWW.SPIRITUALMINDSET.NET

Website: WWW.IMUNLIMITED.NET

CPSIA information can be obtained at www.ICGtesting.com
Printed in the USA
LVOW012019100513

333181LV00013BA/17/P